DEEPER DATING

DEEPER DATING

How to Drop the Games of Seduction
and Discover the Power of Intimacy

KEN PAGE, LCSW

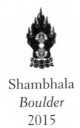

Shambhala
Boulder
2015

Shambhala Publications, Inc.
4720 Walnut Street
Boulder, Colorado 80301
www.shambhala.com

Poem on page 194 reprinted from *Call Me By My True Name* (1999)
by Thich Nhat Hahn with permission of Parallax Press.

9 8 7 6 5 4

Printed in the United States of America

♾This edition is printed on acid-free paper that meets the American National Standards Institute Z39.48 Standard. ♻This book is printed on 30% postconsumer recycled paper. For more information please visit www.shambhala.com.

Distributed in the United States by Penguin Random House LLC
and in Canada by Random House of Canada Ltd

Designed by James D. Skatges

Library of Congress Cataloging-in-Publication Data
Page, Ken, 1956–
Deeper dating: how to drop the games of seduction and discover
the power of intimacy / Ken Page, LCSW. — First edition.
       pages   cm
Includes bibliographical references and index.
ISBN 978-1-61180-122-4 (pbk.: alk. paper)
1. Intimacy (Psychology) 2. Man-woman relationships.
3. Interpersonal relations. 4. Dating (Social customs) I. Title.
BF575.I5P34 2015
646.7'7—dc23
2014007483

To my family and my friends.
You've made me such a lucky man.

Contents

Introduction

The New Map to Love

When I fall in love, it will be forever
Or I'll never fall in love.
— *"When I Fall in Love,"*
VICTOR YOUNG AND EDWARD HEYMAN

I've always loved the song "When I Fall in Love." Its childlike certainty is haunting and wise, but it certainly hasn't been *my* story. And perhaps it hasn't been yours. For most of us, the search for love has been anything but simple. And it's no wonder—we've been handed a map to love that guides us *away* from true intimacy. What do I mean when I say this? Look at the cover of almost any of the magazines that claim to help with dating. What are they telling you to do? Lose weight, dress better, play hard to get, act confident, get out there more—in other words, *fix* yourself if you ever hope to find love. That's not self-improvement. That's self-punishment in camouflage. And self-punishment doesn't lead to healthy love. Instead of helping us to embrace our true selves, the singles world teaches us to improve our packaging. When we finally pause long enough to stop blaming ourselves for our imperfections, we see that this approach ultimately fails.

Think about it: Are the young, gorgeous, witty people you know really more likely to be in healthy, loving relationships? I very much doubt it. Because those aren't the traits that lead to lasting love! More dates? Probably. More opportunities for sex? Almost definitely. But lasting love? Not at all.

The path to a loving relationship is about something much more profound, essential, and life changing than we have ever been taught. The real search for love is about embracing our most authentic self, sharing that true self with the precious people who know how to honor it, and learning to offer others the same in return. The amazing paradox is that the parts of our personality we think we must *fix* in order to find love are usually the *keys* to finding that love. On the path you'll be taking, the focus won't be on fixing yourself; it will be on honoring and expressing your innate gifts. And that changes everything. Instead of holding the whip of self-improvement over yourself, as many of us have spent so much time doing, you will learn to value, trust, and express what I call your Core Gifts.

What are Core Gifts? They are simply your points of deepest sensitivity to life. You will find them in the things that inspire you most, the things that touch you most deeply—and in the things that hurt you the most. Often we think we need to conceal these vulnerable parts of ourselves, to hide them or fix them in order to make ourselves more attractive, but the absolute reverse is true: they are the bullet train to authentic intimacy. When we learn to lead with our Core Gifts, our lives shift on their very axes. Our personal magnetism becomes stronger. We experience more passion and more connection to ourselves and others. Most important, we move closer to the love that may have previously eluded us, a love that empowers us and brings us joy.

I wish that someone had been able to explain this to me during my many years of seeking love. I lost so many years searching for love by trying to change myself into something more "marketable." I can't begin to calculate the number of hours I spent looking for love in environments that lacked love, using methods that had nothing to do with love. Play it cool. Act witty. Swallow all hints of unseemly need.

During those many decades of what I've called my "chronic singlehood," my biggest fear was that I would go through life without ever finding real love. Throughout my twenties, my longest relationships could be measured in months. Too many nights of searching ended with me at the diner, eating my consolation cheeseburger deluxe. My dating life improved as I began to get help from wise friends and skilled therapists, but even so, healthy love evaded me. Whatever the relationship gene was, I was pretty sure I lacked it. By this time I was an experienced, well-regarded psychotherapist, but still, somewhere deep down, I believed some of the biggest cultural myths about how to find love—and I always fell short.

And it wasn't just me. As I continued to struggle to find love, I worked with countless single people in my psychotherapy practice who were coming up against the same disappointments and insecurities.

- "I feel like a sneaker in a dryer. I meet someone new and get lifted up with hope, and then I get dumped down again into the same old dating hell I was in before."

- "After three divorces, in my late sixties, I believe my odds of finding real love are terrible. Flawed merchandise—that's what I feel like."

- "My mom points to her houseplants and tells her friends, 'These are my grandchildren.' I'm a successful attorney with a great life, but in my mother's eyes, and in my own, I feel like a failure because I am single."

Like a number of my clients, I felt as though there was a fatal flaw in my basic wiring. Why did I keep falling for people who weren't good for me? And why did available, kind, thoughtful people make me want to run for the hills? Why did the ones I wanted most never want me back, while those who pursued me barely interested me at all? At some point along the way, this endless cycle of hope and disappointment hit me right between the eyes. I realized that I had spent years *seeking* love, but never working to build it.

I began to look for deeper answers, hoping to unravel the bewildering repetition of dating failures that made up my love life and those of so many others. I sought the help of therapists, friends, and coaches. And I learned so much. Over many years of study, struggle, and growth, I came to realize that there is a path that leads not only to healthy love but to our own personal healing. It is the path of our gifts. It turns out that the qualities I tried so hard to *cover up* in order to attract love were the very things that would *lead* me to my partner and to a life that is rich with intimacy.

As I've learned my lessons about love, I've also taught them. In 2005, after leading many seminars and retreats on intimacy and the search for love, I created a workshop called Deeper Dating, in which single people met in an environment that encouraged kindness, self-discovery, laughter, and discussion. Thousands of single people of all ages, backgrounds, and sexual orientations attended these workshops and many told me how glad they were to have a singles event that left them feeling better about themselves, not worse. The lectures I gave at these events led to opportunities to write for *Psychology Today* and the *Huffington Post*, and the wonderful response I got from those articles fueled my desire to write this book.

Now when I teach the lessons of Deeper Dating, I am invariably met with smiles of recognition and tears of relief. I've seen people's dating lives change dramatically, almost miraculously, when they practice these skills of true intimacy in their search for love.

LONGING FOR LOVE IS WISDOM, NOT WEAKNESS

Of all the harmful myths we're fed, one of the most insidious is the belief that longing for love is a weakness. I disagree. Longing for love is not weakness. It's wisdom. Numbing our loneliness is a path to a despair that plagues our entire culture. We are not meant to be alone and self-sufficient. Without lives filled with love, we wither inside. Intimacy is oxygen. We don't need to transcend our hunger for love—we need to honor it.

According to the psychologist Eli Finkel, one of the most respected researchers in the field of relationships and attraction, the quality of your intimate relationship is one of the greatest determinants of your physical and emotional well-being.[1] This confirms what you've felt all along: finding love matters greatly. Simply holding a loved one's hand lowers blood pressure and reduces pain.[2] What could speak more powerfully about our need for connection than this piece of poetry in scientific form?

I've found that the people who feel they *need* intimacy are the ones who are most likely to find it. If you long for a love that's both kind and passionate, congratulate yourself for being brave enough and determined enough to actually search for it. I invite you to see your longing as a voice of courageous wisdom, not a sign of weakness.

I've seen people just diagnosed with terminal illnesses find love for the first time in their lives, because the burning truth of their mortality finally made them face how important love was to them. I've seen people in their nineties, frail and infirm, experience the giddy thrill of falling in love as a result of their choice to open themselves to intimacy.

And I've seen it in my own life. My relentless desire for love has been the catalyst for so much positive change. It has forced me to admit that I was pushing love away even as I searched for it—and to change those patterns with the help of caring mentors. Those hard-work changes are what enabled me to create the loving life I have today—and to create this new map to love that has helped so many people find the intimacy they yearn for.

NO EMPTY PROMISES

In *Deeper Dating* you won't find a word of advice on how to dress better, flirt better, appear more confident, or keep your partner guessing. (And you wouldn't want my advice anyway—I always failed miserably at these gimmicks!) I also won't promise you love in three months—or in any other time frame. That promise can't be kept and, personally, I don't trust anyone who claims it can. There is a mystery to how and when love is found, and that mystery is ultimately not under our control. The world keeps telling us we need *tricks* to find love. And yes, those tricks work if you're looking for sex or a new relationship with a weak foundation. But they probably won't bring you any closer to finding real love.

As much as we are led to believe that finding love is all about improving ourselves, it's ultimately our *humanity* that lets us find and nurture real love. But don't take my word for it. Try out the ideas in this book, and you will see changes in your life that will prove the power of your own gifts.

This book is for anyone who is single, and for anyone who wants a deeper understanding of the true roots of intimacy. It is for men and women of all ages, backgrounds, sexual orientations, and gender identities. No matter what your age, income, or life circumstances, there are wonderful people out there who are waiting to find someone like you.

The true journey to love takes place on two terrains: the inner and the outer level. Both are necessary, but the essential inner work has been all but ignored in our culture. You can think of this book as a map to both terrains: a guidebook for the most important journey of your life, your journey toward intimacy. This course-in-a-book has the potential to point you toward real love—and toward its source within you. I think you will love what happens, because when you share your deepest gifts with bravery, generosity, and discrimination, love *is* what happens.

How to Speed Your Path to Love

There is a candle in your heart, ready to be kindled.
There is a void in your soul, ready to be filled.
You feel it, don't you?

—RUMI

Welcome to the beginning of your Deeper Dating journey. In the weeks ahead you will come to see your search for love in a new way and learn intimacy tools you've probably never been taught. In this approach, your focus won't be on repairing your flaws; it will be on embracing your Core Gifts, the most defining qualities of your being. This gift-based approach to intimacy is not just a strategy to hook a mate—it is the path to a richer life.

The Deeper Dating course follows four stages. Each stage is composed of two to four lessons, and every chapter constitutes one full lesson. I suggest that you take one week for each chapter. In the future, you can always redo any chapters that feel important, or retake the entire course.

THE FOUR STAGES OF THE DEEPER DATING JOURNEY

In the first stage (chapters 1 to 3) you will discover some of your most essential Core Gifts. You will come to understand how they have shaped your entire romantic history—and how they can lead you to the love you are looking for. As you discover and embrace your Core Gifts you will feel both stronger and more comfortable with your vulnerability. From that foundation, your search for love will begin to change in wonderful ways. Starting with the first chapter, you'll learn new dating skills so that you can begin making concrete changes from the very beginning of this course.

In Stage 2 (chapters 4 to 6) you'll learn what I consider the single most important dating tool: distinguishing between your "attractions of inspiration," the attractions that are most likely to lead to lasting love, and your "attractions of deprivation," those that draw you in and lead you to replay old, painful relationship patterns. You'll create a clear portrait of both of these attractions. And you'll learn how even your most painful attractions can lead you to your deepest gifts. You'll learn an exquisite and powerful five-minute process to help you to connect to the source of love inside you.

In Stage 3 (chapters 7 to 10) you'll learn the actual skills of Deeper Dating. You'll bring the unique gifts of your authentic self into your real-world dating life—online, at parties and dating events, and in day-to-day life. You'll learn about the single greatest saboteur of healthy love and discover the ways you may be pushing intimacy away without realizing it. And you'll learn how to bring hope and growth to the challenging middle phase of your journey to find love.

In Stage 4 (chapters 11 and 12) you'll learn how to build sexual, romantic, and emotional intimacy in the new healthy relationships you'll be finding. Passion and intimacy grow very differently in healthy relationships than in unhealthy ones—you'll learn how to nurture both of these qualities in a safe and stable love. You'll also discover your unique sexual and romantic Core Gifts.

Within a matter of weeks of starting the Deeper Dating course you may well start to notice wonderful differences. You may feel more comfortable in your own skin. You'll probably begin to find your dating life reshaping itself in ways that excite and challenge you. In less time than you might imagine, you may find yourself dating people who are kinder, more available, and more accepting of you. You'll gradually find your taste for unavailable people diminishing, and your appreciation for kindness, generosity, authenticity, and availability growing. These changes happen because you're learning the life-affirming lessons of true intimacy—not the dehumanizing games of seduction.

DEEPER DATING: AN INTIMACY-BASED APPROACH

One of the definitions of the word *intimate* is "belonging to or characterizing one's deepest nature." I believe that this is the heart of intimacy: connecting with your own deepest nature, and sharing it with bravery and generosity with the people who deserve that privilege. Intimacy can be thought of as "into-me-see": the process of seeing into our loved one and allowing him or her to do the same with us.

In his book *Touching: The Human Significance of the Skin*, Ashley Montagu explains that when certain mammals are born, their mother must lick them all over. If certain important body parts are not licked, the internal organs corresponding to that part of the animal's body may never function properly. The baby's organs need to be "seen and touched" if they are ever to function fully.[1]

This illustrates one of the great secrets of our gifts. When someone recognizes our gifts, those gift are given license to come alive, to become generous, expressive, and brave. The truth is, we need each other in order to grow—and to learn.

That is why I'm going to encourage you to *study* this course in a way that includes as much support and dialogue as possible. You can read this book on your own and still benefit greatly from it. However, if you discuss your experiences in this course with friends, loved ones, or with a learning partner, the benefits will be even more powerful. (I'll describe what I mean by a learning partner in the next section of this chapter.) The research is more than clear on this: most of us learn more effectively and enjoyably when we learn with others.[2] Learning to embrace our Core Gifts is hard to accomplish alone. Changing the behaviors that keep us from love is almost *impossible* to accomplish alone. Love is built, and born, in the mistakes and corrections we make; in the breaking and repairing, the hurt and the healing. In the coming weeks, half of your learning will come from your mistakes and through the correction of those mistakes. For such learning to happen, the support of others makes a huge difference.

I believe that the ideas in this book have the power to lead you to love and to profoundly enrich your life. But conversation, support, and guidance will help make them come to life for you. With the help and support of people you trust,

- You'll grow to appreciate your gifts more and more.

- You'll learn the lessons in this book on a deeper level, and you'll be more likely to keep using them after you have finished the book.

- When things go well, you'll have a cheering squad. When things are rough, you'll have a problem-solving team.

A number of years ago, two friends and I—three "chronically single psychotherapists"—started a support group. Week after week we met and supported one another as we encountered the ongoing challenges of our dating lives. Left to our own devices, we would have made the same habitual choices we'd made in the past—and ended up with the same disappointments. Now, with one another's help, we found escape routes out of our unhelpful patterns. As a result, the new choices we made held the lovely taste of earned wisdom. That group changed my dating life. And each one of us— after a combined count of many decades of singlehood—is now in a great relationship.

Your Learning Partner

One of the best ways to take this course is with a learning partner. A learning partner is a co-coach in this defining life journey. Your learning partner relationship will be an important one for you, so choose well. He or she must be someone who will keep your secrets secret. Someone who can bring a sense of hope to your shared journey. Someone who is both emotionally safe and insightful.

How do you find such a person? This in itself is an important intimacy lesson. My assumption is that you have more potential support in your life than you realize. That's the best place to start. Look at your contact lists from the past few years, and ask yourself these questions:

- Who is kind?

- Who has wisdom?

- Who is essentially reliable, and really cares about you?

Highlight each person's name. They are your dream team in life. And any one of them who is single can be your learning partner. When you find your learning partner, and when you both agree to take this journey together, you can use the exercises at the end of each chapter as a study and discussion guide.

If you don't have someone in mind, stay open to possibilities. In the meantime, look on the Deeper Dating website to find webinars, discussions, and classes. Some of these classes will match you with a learning partner. You can also start your own Deeper Dating study group with as few or as many people as you wish. You can meet weekly or biweekly, share your experiences, and complete the workbook exercises for each chapter.

Your Deeper Dating Workbook

At the end of each chapter is a workbook section with exercises that will help bring these ideas to life for you. There are personal exercises for you to do on your own, exercises to do with your learning partner, and Deeper Dating exercises designed to help you make concrete changes in your dating life. I encourage you to take the time to complete these exercises. They will enrich all the work you've done in the chapter.

Micro-meditations

The exercises at the end of each chapter will make these ideas come to life for you. But what about the moments of insight you have *while* you're reading a chapter? By the time you go back to the exercises, those moments will have passed. That's why I have put micro-meditations, each of which takes no more than a few minutes, in the body of each chapter. Try to do them as you read instead of putting them off for later. You'll love how just a few minutes of practicing a micro-meditation can deepen and enrich the way you feel.

These micro-meditations can be done by anyone, even those of us with constantly wandering minds. Don't worry if you can hold an instruction for only a moment before it dissipates. That's fine. If that moment touches you, the micro-meditation has done its job. Don't worry if your micro-meditations run faster or slower than the suggested time. Follow your own pacing.

Your Journal

Find a pleasing journal or an electronic device for the writing exercises you'll be doing as part of this course. Many new insights and ideas will be coming to you in the weeks ahead. Your journal will be a home for these insights, and a place to come back to when you need a dose of your own wisdom.

LEARNING THROUGH PLEASURE

One of the best ways to digest the concepts in this book is to simply savor those parts that hit home for you. The ideas, stories, and exercises were designed to bring you into contact with the warm humanity of your own Core Gifts, the resonance of your own deep insights. If anything touches you in a visceral way, just put the book down for a moment. Let the ripples of your emotion or insight do their work inside you and allow yourself to take pleasure in that experience. By honoring your pacing and your experience, you'll be living from your gifts as you read. Many of the messages in this book—such as learning to discover your greatest gifts within your deepest insecurities—are different from ideas you've been taught in the past. You may want to make notes, highlight passages, and keep the book nearby as you're taking this course.

Finally, practice gentleness with yourself. This course will ask you to touch the deepest roots of your being, and that is an act of bravery. When you hit bewilderment in your journey (and you will—after all, we're talking about *dating* here!) try to be kind to yourself. You may find yourself still going back to old patterns, but recognize that every bit of new behavior will have positive ripples in your life. Progress is always imperfect, and the skills we learn from our errors are usually invaluable.

YOUR FIRST DEEPER DATING MICRO-MEDITATION
Beginning Your Journey | Two minutes

You're about to embark upon a journey toward real love, through practicing the skills of true intimacy. I invite you to acknowledge yourself for taking this step.

Think of a few of the people who have loved you most. They may be alive or not, but they are still close to your heart—and they would want the best for you, including a relationship that brings you happiness. Take a moment to picture each of them. Would any of them have words of support or advice for you as you begin this journey? Visualize their faces as you imagine what each one might say to you. Then, internally thank them. Take a gentle breath in, then exhale and let their support infuse you.

Deeper Dating Workbook

Important Note: Please note that many of the exercises and approaches in this book work for many people, but they will not work, and may even exacerbate problems in harmful ways, if untreated or undertreated emotional or psychological disorders are present, or if a person has an active addiction. If you have an addiction or a psychiatric condition that's getting in the way of your life, please seek the help of a licensed mental health professional, a twelve-step program, or other appropriate help and address these issues *before* beginning this course. No matter how much the ideas in this book ring true for you, you'll keep sabotaging all your potential success in innumerable ways if you don't address these issues first. Without that support, the deep work you'll be doing in this course may also be harmful or destabilizing.

PERSONAL EXERCISES
Write Your Own Mission Statement

You are now going to write a very important paragraph: a mission statement for your journey to find your beloved. Sit down with your new journal in a comfortable place. Take a few moments for each of these thought exercises:

1. Think of a few of the moments of the deepest intimacy in your life. (Think of all kinds of love, not just romantic love, and only choose memories that occurred with someone whom you still trust and feel safe with.) Remember how it felt to experience such deep closeness with another.

2. Picture your future with a loving partner and all the family of friends and loved ones that could surround you. Remember why finding a life partner and building a family matter so much to you.

3. Now, write one paragraph on why it matters so much to take this journey at this point in your life. Let yourself speak from the urgency and passion you're feeling. When you finish, sign and date your entry.

This mission statement is a declaration of your goals, a restatement of why you're taking this journey into Deeper Dating. Copy it and carry it in your wallet or purse. Place it in a visible spot. Every now and then read it again, and let its importance and truth ripple through you. You might even wish to write yourself a letter with your mission statement, then stamp and mail it to yourself for a lovely reminder.

Find a Learning Partner or Other Support

As you move into this new paradigm of Deeper Dating, you'll have many opportunities to practice bravery. Here's the first: Find support; don't start alone. Following are three options for finding that support. Aim as high as you can, but do not punish yourself for a step you aren't ready to take:

1. Find a learning partner and begin the course together.

2. Find at least one friend who agrees to occasionally speak with you and offer support as you progress in this course, even if he is not following this course. Optimally, you can offer your friend the same support for any endeavor he is committed to. Alternatively, find support through the Deeper Dating website or a coach who will support you in this process.

3. Read and savor this book, doing whichever exercises you like. You'll still get great value from it. You can find a learning partner or other support at any point along the way if you decide you want to.

DEEPER DATING EXERCISE
Notice Your Patterns

For your first Deeper Dating exercise, just notice your patterns of behavior in your search for intimacy. Don't try to make any changes. You may be dating a lot or not at all. You may have specific places where you try to meet people, and ways of interacting when you meet them. Just notice your patterns with a sense of nonjudgmental curiosity. The more you notice now, the more clarity you will have as things change for you. Make a few short notes on the patterns you notice.

LEARNING PARTNER EXERCISE
Plan Your Meetings

When you find your learning partner, if you choose to work with one, make a plan to meet or talk on a regular basis, according to your schedules. You should meet for at least 30 minutes for each new chapter, and more if you like. Your first exercise will begin in chapter 1.

Discover Your Unique Core Gifts

In the next three chapters you will develop a more intimate understanding of the self you love *from*. Your Core Gifts are the parts of you that respond most intensely to love—and to the hurts and joys that surround love. They are the parts of yourself where you *care* about intimacy most deeply. Your Core Gifts are an essential key to finding and keeping love. They hold your personal magic. In this first stage you'll discover your Gift Zone, the zone where you are in living contact with your Core Gifts. You will begin to explore one of life's most profound mysteries: how our deepest wounds spring from our most essential gifts. You'll learn how to find your Core Gifts, and reclaim them from the wounds and insecurities that keep them buried. This relationship with your authentic self will form the foundation of your whole Deeper Dating journey.

The Old Map to Love

Attractiveness comes first if you want to find your mate. The younger and more beautiful you are, the more perfect your body and more compelling your style, the easier it is to find love. Attractiveness comes first and the rest follows.

The New Map to Love

Take a guess: Which quality do people rate as the most desirable in a mate, across cultures, ages, and genders? It is not success. It is not attractiveness. It is not wittiness. The evolutionary psychologist David Buss conducted an extensive study of the traits people rate as most important in finding a mate, and his finding was clear. Number one is kindness and understanding.[1] It's not that looks don't matter—they do. But their role in finding lasting, healthy love has been vastly overemphasized. In fact, research strongly suggests that people who are extremely attractive are no more likely to find lasting love than people who are of average attractiveness.[2] Why has no one told us this?

This is powerful news. It means the more we learn the skills of authentic intimacy, the more desirable we become. It means those extra pounds might not matter as much as your open heart. That simply showing more warmth and interest on your next date might pay off better than all those extra hours spent in pursuit of six-pack abs. It's not surprising that kindness is also the key to making your next relationship flourish. According to the researcher Arthur Aron, "kindness is the strongest indicator for a successful long-term relationship."[3]

1

Your Gift Zone

The Birthplace of Intimacy

And we are put on earth a little space,
That we may learn to bear the beams of love
—WILLIAM BLAKE

Each of us has unique qualities of sensitivity, parts of ourselves where we feel most intensely and care most deeply. I call these places of deepest sensitivity our Core Gifts. When our Core Gifts are touched, our reactions have a greater charge than usual; we may feel deeply inspired, highly emotional, or surprisingly hurt. Our Core Gifts are as unique and as universal as our own fingerprints, and they lie at the heart of our entire intimacy journey.

Core Gifts are not the same as talents or skills; in fact, until we understand them, our Core Gifts are often the very qualities we're most ashamed of, the ones we keep trying to fix or hide because they make us feel so vulnerable. Yet they are also the places from which we love most fully. There is a formula that I've seen proven true in my work and my life: to the degree that we treasure our Core Gifts (yes, treasure them; dispassionate acceptance isn't enough) we attract caring, thoughtful people who are also (miracle of miracles) attracted to us. And, equally amazing, we become more attracted to people who are good for us, and less interested in people who diminish us or leave us feeling insecure.

However, the opposite is also true: to the degree that we distance ourselves from our gifts, we become attracted to people who are unavailable or who can't love us for who we are. And we find ourselves *less* attracted to available people who value us for who we are.

HOW YOUR DEEPEST INSECURITIES
REVEAL YOUR GREATEST GIFTS

Through decades of practice as a psychotherapist, and from a lifetime of efforts to understand my own inner workings, something surprising and inspiring gradually became clear to me: our deepest wounds surround our greatest gifts.

I've found that the very qualities we're most ashamed of, the ones we keep trying to reshape or hide, are in many ways the key to finding real love. Deep inside we know that these Core Gifts are worthy, and we never stop longing to find someone who treasures them, but after getting the message that these gifts are risky or unlovable, we learn to hide and bury them.

Over the years I realized that the characteristics of my clients that I found most inspiring—that were most essentially "them"—were the ones that frequently caused them the most suffering.

Some clients would complain of feeling that they were "too much": too intense, too angry, or too demanding. From my therapist's chair, I would see a passion so powerful that it frightened people away.

Other clients said they felt like they were "not enough": too weak, too quiet, too ineffective. I would find a quality of humility and grace in them that prevented them from asserting themselves as others did.

Clients would describe lives devastated by codependency, and I would see an immense generosity with no healthy limits.

Again and again, where my clients saw their greatest wounds I saw their defining gifts. And I saw the same dynamic in my own life.

For most of my adult life I was chronically single. Contrary to every bit of personal growth work I had done, somewhere inside I still believed that if I really wanted to find love, it all came down to getting in shape and becoming more confident. I believed that the "flaws" in my body and my being were what kept me from finding love. On those rare occasions that I hit my goals for a buff body and perfect weight, I was thrilled to be approached more often. I had more sex and more dates. But the degree of intimacy in my dating life remained completely unchanged. In the end, my physique and my ability to find lasting love had precisely *nothing* to do with each other. Zero. Whether buff and toned, or not, I remained attracted to the bad-boy type, and I continued to be turned off by guys who were kind, available, and interested in me. I kept trying to find love in the same ways, and the frustration and futility of my efforts forced me to find help in therapy.

It was in therapy that I discovered my Core Gift of tenderness — and confronted how angry and ashamed that gift made me feel. I grew up in a family of Holocaust survivors. In their eyes, too much tenderness translated into weakness, and weakness led to death. So I grew up with a powerful wall of shame and anger around this central attribute of my being. And that wall stopped me from finding any lasting romantic relationship. Until I was far into my twenties, six weeks was the marker of my longest relationship.

Through therapy I also recognized my sensitivity to others' pain or joy, a quality that I had always loved in myself. However, that didn't stop me from throwing my sensitivity right under the bus in order to look more confident. I began to realize that there was a self inside me that I had been picking at, cutting at, and trying to secretly drown. My problem, as I saw it, was that it wouldn't die gently! I couldn't live with my deepest gifts, but I couldn't live without them, either. Down to my bones, I thought that my sensitivity was my weakness. It wasn't. *My weakness was my lack of respect for that sensitivity.* What I know now is that those troublesome, passionate, *different* qualities were the very best part of me. I just hadn't been taught how to walk past the tangles of shame that surrounded them.

As I came to value my sensitivity (a journey that still continues), my life began to change in wonderful ways. I started *building* love, not just chasing it down with people who weren't particularly interested. I began to spend time with the precious people who honored me for who I was. I gradually stopped looking for tawdry sex and found myself meeting kind and available men more often. The more I embraced my authentic self, the more the quality of men I dated improved.

Finally, at the age of fifty-one, I met my partner, Greg, a person who is extremely kind, consistently loving, and generous of spirit. He has a quality of essential goodness and rock-solid caring that just makes me want to celebrate. And I am certain of this: in the past I would have fled him a thousand times over. Love would have been right in front of me. But, filled with loneliness, hunting compulsively for my next date, I would have passed Greg right by.

Excited by the possibilities of all that I was learning, I began to formulate a system to help people discover their own Core Gifts and work with them to create love and deeper meaning in their lives. I call this system Gift Theory.

GIFT THEORY AND THE ZONES OF INTIMACY

The easiest way to explain Gift Theory and to help you begin to get a sense of your Core Gifts is by starting with an image of a target (see diagram 1). This target image will be your map throughout this entire course. It points the way to intimacy by pointing the way to *you*. On this "target of intimacy" the closer you are to the center, the closer you come to your most authentic self. The inner circle of the target is your Gift Zone. It is the seat of true intimacy. (In fact, the word *intimate* comes from the Latin word *intimus*, which means "innermost.")

Our Core Gifts hold the key to ourselves and our relationships. But they can scare us. It takes work to learn to handle their complexity, vulnerability, and power. As worthy as our gifts are, they are by no means hall passes to happiness. They get us into trouble again and again. We become most defensive, or most

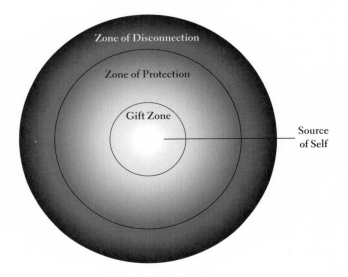

Diagram 1: Your Zones of Intimacy

naive, around them. They challenge us and the people we care about. They ask more of us than we want to give. And we can be devastated when we feel them betrayed or rejected. (In chapter 2 we will explore why this is so.)

Since the heat of our core is so hard to handle, we protect ourselves by moving further out from the center. Each step we take away from the center of the circle represents a more airbrushed version of ourselves. Each zone outward makes us feel safer, puts us at less risk of embarrassment, failure, and rejection. Yet each zone outward also moves us one step further from our soul, our authenticity, and our sense of meaning. As we get further away from our Core Gifts, we feel more and more alone and adrift. When we get too far from the warmth and humanity of our deepest self, we begin to experience a very painful sense of emptiness and despair.

Most of us set up shop at a point where we are close enough to be warmed by our gifts but far enough away that we don't get burned by their fire. We create safer versions of ourselves in order to get through our lives without having to face the existential risk of our core. Unfortunately, our core is where we love *from*. Our task now is to get *closer* to the inner circle of our being—and to be able to share our Core Gifts with increasing wisdom, bravery, generosity, and discrimination.

The target diagram has three concentric rings that represent the three main zones of intimacy. Let's take a look at each zone in more detail, so that you can connect this map to the realities of your own life.

Zone 1: The Gift Zone

Zone 1 is the bull's eye, your Gift Zone. Whenever you feel the warmth of your humanity and hold it with a sense of compassion or care, you are in your Gift Zone. The great Christian mystic Meister Eckhart said that the way to create a perfect circle is always to begin with the center. Your Gift Zone is your center. If this entire book had to be reduced to one lesson, it would be to live more of your life in this zone. In it you are connected with your Core Gifts. From here you find your greatest capacity to connect with another. Have you ever felt a strong sense of connection to your innermost self? Or to that of someone else? In those moments, you are in your Gift Zone. Here are some examples of being in your Gift Zone:

- Feeling moved by a story, an insight, or a piece of art or music
- Feeling a wordless ache in your heart
- Being touched by something beautiful in nature
- Feeling a wave of longing for something or someone
- The feeling of holding hands with someone you love
- The feeling of pleasure in helping someone
- Feeling love for a person or a pet who also loves you

Does anything on this list hit home for you? Let's do a micro-meditation to help you connect to your Gift Zone.

MICRO-MEDITATION

Your Gift Zone | Two minutes

Think back to a time when you experienced a rich sense of connection to the warmth of your own humanity. Read the examples in the list above and see what memories they trigger for you. Choose a memory that stands out. (It doesn't need to be big or dramatic.) Go back and remember the experience you chose. Where were you at the time? What was happening? Try to recall how the event unfolded, and the feelings it evoked in you. Remember how that experience touched you.

Now just savor that memory of being in your Gift Zone. Take a gentle breath in and out. Hold the feeling close, and see if you can let it linger just a bit as you continue reading.

Your Gift Zone is your springboard to intimacy and to the love you are looking for. *The more you live in your Gift Zone and act on its promptings, the more love you will have in your life—and the closer you will come to your future relationship.* In this zone your unique magic comes alive and begins to influence your world.

How do you access the Gift Zone? By noticing whatever you feel in the moment and holding that feeling with compassion. The more you feel your authentic experience with a sense of compassion and honor, the closer you are to your Gift Zone. In a way, that's a simple definition of intimacy: authenticity plus compassion. The easiest way to get to your Gift Zone is through the moments in your life when your heart feels touched or you feel inspired. Most of us have at least some of them every day, but we haven't been taught to see them as portals to deeper intimacy. When we have these moments of inspiration—no matter how small—we can stay with them for a few extra beats and just savor them. In doing this, we taste their deeper flavor, and at that point, we are in our Gift Zone.

It is much harder to stay in the Gift Zone if you are feeling anger or pain. At those times it's easier to shut your heart to the hurt, or to want to hurt back, or to become angry at yourself. But it is very possible to remain in the Gift Zone even in pain, sadness, or anger; it just requires a greater amount of skill and compassion to stay connected to the warmth of your humanity in those times.

Your Gift Zone isn't static. It is constantly generating a living stream of impulses toward intimacy and authentic self-expression. It *wants* things. It reaches for life. It needs to connect—and it tells you how. In your Gift Zone you might feel a desire to listen to a piece of music or to go for a walk, to be alone or to reach out to someone. Your intimacy journey becomes an adventure when you act on the promptings of your Gift Zone. Doing so will change your love life from the inside out. It will begin a wave of unknotting and self-expression that will ripple into the ways you love and the way you live.

The closer to the center of the target we get, the deeper we enter into our Gift Zone. If we follow it inward, ever deeper, to the very core of our being, we come to the very center of the circle, which I call the "Source of Self." Because this is the core of our very being, it is precious and life-filled. This is the state where the personal touches something greater, where we feel awe or a sense of indescribable connection to something vast. We can call it God or higher power or human goodness or simply the great mystery. Each of us has our own language for it. Whether we are atheist, agnostic, spiritual, or religious, this Source of Self is part of the gift of being human. Our Gift Zone is a portal to this magnificent state.

When we're in the Gift Zone we hold a certain luminosity. Even in sadness we are somehow lit from within, because we are holding our experience with a quality of compassion. This is the zone that attracts love. And like anything that precious, the stakes get raised if we want to claim it. Claiming our authentic self is one of the scariest and most heroic things we can do. In our Gift Zone, there's a sense of aliveness, a sense of *self*—even if that sense of self doesn't feel as secure or happy as we think it should. We brave a new frontier when we face the risk of entering our Gift Zone. And that very sense of risk heightens our ability to love.

The study "Love on a Suspension Bridge" by the researchers Arthur Aron and Donald G. Dutton shows how risk and attraction are linked. In the study, female interviewers approached men who were walking across two different bridges. One bridge was a wobbly wooden suspension bridge swaying 230 feet above a river. The other bridge was lower and more stable, and crossed over a peaceful stream. The men on the scary, high bridge were more likely to find the female interviewers attractive, and to contact them after the experiment ended, than were the men on the lower bridge. The researchers surmised that the men on the high bridge associated the heightened arousal brought on by being in a risky situation with the person they were meeting. In addition, they believed that this experience may have triggered the desire for self-expansion, a broadening of self through deeper connection with others.[1] Why did the higher bridge trigger a desire for self-expansion? In my opinion, it is because when we're in the presence of risk, thrill, or inspiration, we are closer to the existential aliveness of our Gift Zone. In that zone, perched between fear and exhilaration, we are more likely to feel the urgent importance of love. We all have a suspension bridge inside us that we can visit anytime we wish: it is the scary challenge of authenticity. If we seek deeper intimacy in our lives, each of us must face inward to the challenge of our authentic self.

The next time you are in your Gift Zone, try staying with it for an extra moment. Chances are great that you will have a small swell of feeling, a sense of inner richness. Allow yourself to savor that feeling as it moves through you and then passes. You don't have to do anything more. Simply appreciating the feeling will deepen and enrich you, and make room for it to come up more frequently. This tiny practice makes us warmer and more accessible to love.

Two things are needed to find access to this magic zone: a willingness to see and feel whatever is in our heart at the moment, and a simple honoring of those feelings, whatever they are. The psychotherapist Patricia Simko says, "Follow whatever you are feeling,

welcoming everything, shunning nothing. Follow every crenella-
tion of the coastline of your being, and you will find a portal to your
greater self."[2] We can't locate our gifts if we're not authentic, and
we can't see their beauty and worth without compassion. Authenticity is your key to enter the Gift Zone. Compassion is what turns
the lights on to let you see your gifts.

Sometimes what we feel in our Gift Zone may be hard to bear.
Remember: You don't have to immerse yourself fully in a feeling to
be in your Gift Zone. It is enough to stand as close as you can to the
heat of your authenticity. Eugene T. Gendlin, the influential psychotherapist who developed the technique called Focusing, expressed this idea in a humorous way: "If you want to smell the soup,
you don't stick your head in it."[3] Imagine sleeping with your loved
one, just touching shoulders as you sleep, barely knowing it but
somehow feeling comforted by that touch. As with that lover, lightly
touching your Gift Zone is enough for the flowering of self to occur.
Immersion is often not even necessary.

Your Gift Zone carries magic because it springs from the source
of your true self. Your song, should you be brave enough to sing it,
will attract people who are searching for someone like you. As you
live from your Gift Zone, you will meet people you wouldn't have
met. You will create things in the world. You will inspire people.
You will feel strange and scared at times, but you will be claiming
new ground of personal goodness, ground that others will want to
stand on—I promise you. When you live in your Gift Zone, you
will shine. Many people won't notice—and they don't have to. The
people who have been hungry for a person like you will feel thankful that they have finally found you.

Zone 2: The Zone of Protection

As I mentioned earlier, the feeling of vulnerability and risk that
comes with living in our Gift Zone causes most of us to set up shop
in Zone 2, the zone of protection. In this zone, we are far enough
away from the heat of our core that we won't get burned by its fire

and challenge. We create airbrushed versions of ourselves to protect us from living in the existential risk of our core. The more we
do this, the less authentic we become; we may face less risk but we
also create less love.

Sometimes, inhabiting Zone 2 is a conscious choice, like turning on the television to get one's mind off a troubling work problem. It can be a wise thing to do when life becomes too intense or
too hard to bear. A break, a nap, a snack, an entertaining beach
book—enjoying these things is part of what makes us human and
increases our enjoyment of life. All of us flee the depth of our sensitivity, passion, hungers, and hurts, and usually we don't even realize we're doing it. We each have myriad methods for avoiding our
feelings, and evading the things that are most exciting, important,
and scary to us. Often these methods of avoidance can begin to take
over our lives.

Jill craved being home alone every night, surfing online, and
having some wine. She craved it so much that an invitation to a
party would make her uncomfortable. A call at night, even from
someone she loved, would irritate her.

Joel would spend his evenings at home playing games with online friends and strangers. Often, he'd stay up too late and be tired
the next day at work, which would lead him to stay in the next night
and repeat the same pattern.

Here are some more tools of protection:

- Avoiding the search for love

- Online distractions

- Workaholism

- Abusing mood-altering substances

- Romantic obsessions

- Keeping distance from the people and things that matter most
  to us

When our true self feels unsafe in the world, we begin to create a false self that lets us feel safe and accepted—but at significant cost. The less authentic we become, the less we feel our Core Gifts. As our protection intensifies, we begin to enter a state of numbness. Too much of this numbness moves us into the danger zone, Zone 3.

Note that in our diagram, the inner part of Zone 2 is gray, because both our pain and our joy are dulled. As we move toward the outer region of this Zone of Protection, the color becomes darker; now we are beginning to feel the pain of isolation, of disconnection from ourselves and others. Here our protection is beginning to hurt us.

As we move further away from our core, our desire to isolate and our dependency on these tools of protection become stronger and more intense. The further we move into this zone, the more fiercely we protect the very things that are eating away at our humanity from the inside. We become less resilient, less tolerant, and more prone to depression and inner emptiness.

Zone 3: The Zone of Disconnection

The final zone is that of disconnection. In the inner part of this zone—the part closest to the center of the target—existence is still tolerable. But as we move toward the outer edges, the alienation starts to hurt badly. We feel the barren darkness of isolation. A coldness or a deadening emptiness starts to seep into our being. If we find ourselves in this zone, it is usually wise to seek help. At this time, we need to find support from others. If there are any untreated emotional or psychological disorders or active addictions, we must address these quickly. If you feel as though you are in Zone 3, please consider getting professional help. The work of this book is best done when you are not in that zone. Being in it is nothing to be ashamed of. Many of us have spent time in the Zone of Disconnection, and that experience is often one of our greatest spurs to healing and success.

Tracking Your Own Zones of Intimacy

Recently I showed a kid-friendly diagram of the zones of intimacy to my eleven-year-old son. I drew shining hearts in the Gift Zone to signify love, light bulbs to symbolize inspiration, and hearts with arrows in them to symbolize hurt. For the Zone of Protection I wrote the word "numb." For the Zone of Disconnection I wrote the words "pain" and "alone."

He immediately related to the diagram. He pointed to the Zone of Protection and he said, "These are some of my days at school." He pointed to the Zone of Disconnection and said, "This is how I feel if I get teased." Then he went into the Gift Zone. He pointed to the outer part of the Gift Zone, and said, "This is when I'm doing my writing." He then pointed deeper in, close to the center, and said, "This is when I'm doing art and music." And then he took his pen and placed it right in the center and he said, "This is how I feel when I'm petting our cat Mabel." He got it completely.

In your workbook for this lesson, you will have the chance to think about your own personal experience of these zones. The Intimacy Fix taught in this micro-meditation will teach you a quick process to increase the experience of intimacy in your life by moving closer toward your Gift Zone. I invite you to use it as often as you like.

MICRO-MEDITATION

The Intimacy Fix | Three minutes

Take a moment to breathe. Without overthinking it, where would you place yourself on the Zones of Intimacy diagram? Which zone are you in and, within that zone, at what distance from the center would you place yourself? It may be a simple answer or it may be nuanced or unclear. You may be in a few zones at once. Rest with the question and see what answer comes up. If you feel you're in the Gift Zone, celebrate and relish this. Ask what your Gift Zone would like from you right now: a walk, reaching out to a friend, cooking something. See if you can do what it asks. Stay with your experience—you don't need to read on. You're there.

If you're feeling disconnected from your Gift Zone, don't judge yourself. Most of us spend vast amounts of time away from there. But often, we're closer to it than we might think. Picture your Gift Zone and imagine going into it. See what it feels like. If this is hard to do, ask yourself what might help you move closer to it. If you have an insight about what that would be, see if you can act on it. Look at this insight as a small marching order from your intuition. If nothing comes up, that's fine, too. Keep trying this micro-meditation. As you do this exercise more and more often you'll develop a library, a tasting menu, of what brings you into your Gift Zone.

Every time you do this exercise you are deepening your self-love, crowding out your self-critic, and inviting intimacy into your life. Take a step in toward your Gift Zone, just a small one, and watch what happens—because something will. You will feel more enlivened, more challenged, and more authentic. Even if what you feel is painful, if you can put words on it and gently hold it with compassion, it will open you to greater intimacy. In this way you can actually control and modulate the depth of your connection to your deepest self and to others, simply by taking a step inward toward the truth of what you're feeling. The experience of one of my clients captures this beautifully.

Lisa was in bed with Jim after a wonderful evening together. Jim was trying to make the remote work so they could watch a movie. However, Lisa was feeling the need for intimate contact with Jim, so she felt left out in the cold as he gave his full attention to the remote. She began to feel needy, and that made her annoyed with herself—and with him. She felt she had moved to a deeper level of commitment to Jim that night, but she wasn't sure if he felt the same. She wanted them to share closeness, not electronics. Most of all, she was embarrassed by her need. It would have felt way too vulnerable for her to reveal that she needed to be held, or that she wanted reassurance that he felt the same closeness she did. Yet *not* doing so left her feeling alone and resentful.

She tried the intimacy-fix micro-meditation. First, she determined where she was on the target. She decided that she was in the Protection Zone, inching toward the Zone of Disconnection, but she couldn't figure out how to move closer to the Gift Zone. She imagined what her learning partner would suggest to help her to move closer to her Gift Zone. She guessed that her friend would have said, "Ask Jim to put down the remote, and tell him what you're feeling. Tell him how close you're feeling to him, and that you just want to cuddle for now and wait with the movie."

"Ugh," thought Lisa. "Hard. Embarrassing. What a wimp I feel like."

But, having learned the lessons of honoring her vulnerability, Lisa bit the bullet and did this.

Jim was surprised and asked her if he could just finish fixing the remote first. Lisa stayed true to her feelings and said, "I just want to feel your arms around me for a few minutes. Do you mind if we wait with the remote?" Jim's response was wonderful. He put down the remote and they cuddled for a while. She told him what she was feeling, and it made him very happy. For him, it had just been another great date. He wasn't having the same intense experience as Lisa, but he loved that *she* was having it. Lisa's heart felt very full. She could have stayed like that all night, but she knew Jim really wanted to see the movie, so when she was ready, she gave him a squeeze and told him to go ahead with the remote.

Lisa remembered how many times she had been in similar situations and how she would shut down or get angry. Now she knew her gift: how emotionally affected she was by intimacy. She was able to honor her gift, be brave and vulnerable at the same time, and move closer to both her boyfriend and herself.

Deeper Dating Workbook

PERSONAL EXERCISES
Map Your Zones of Intimacy

1. Write one or more memories of being in your Gift Zone.

2. Write down two activities that help you enter your Gift Zone.

3. Write down two people in whose presence you can easily enter into your Gift Zone.

4. List three things you do in your life that you use to move into the Zone of Protection.

5. Remember a time in your life when you were in the Zone of Isolation. What helped you get out of it?

DEEPER DATING EXERCISE
Your Gift Zone and Your Dating Life

This practice will quickly begin to change the tenor of your dating life. If you don't currently have a romantic interest, try practicing it with your friends and loved ones.

When you are on a date or with someone new, notice how you feel in his company. Is it relatively easy to slide into a light state of your Gift Zone with him? If so, that's a very good sign. If not, try practicing the intimacy-fix micro-meditation and see what happens. What shifts occur in your behavior? Do any corresponding shifts occur for the person you're with? Notice how this one shift in your awareness begins to change things on your date. Discuss your experience with your learning partner or a friend.

LEARNING PARTNER EXERCISE
Introduce Yourselves and Take the First Step

At your first meeting, allow each partner to answer these questions:

1. Start by sharing why each of you wants to take this journey at this time in your life What's going on in your dating life at this time? Are there problems or challenges you keep hitting up against, or any areas of growth you are noticing? Share one hope that you each have as you begin this course.

2. Tell each other what you need in your co-coaching relationship. For example, "I've avoided looking for a relationship for years and I'm ready to start again, but I need to feel support—not advice on what to do differently." An equally valid request: "Be honest with me. Let me know what you are seeing, and hold me accountable. I need that now. I've wasted time for too long."

At the end of each talk, plan and confirm your next meeting.

2

Your Core Gifts

A Key to Finding Your Beloved—and Yourself

> Everybody is a genius. But if you judge a fish by its ability to climb a tree, it will live its whole life believing that it is stupid.
> —ORIGIN UNKNOWN (often attributed to Albert Einstein)

Have you discovered the secret to cheating at a maze? Instead of starting from the outside, you begin at the center and work your way out. Working a maze from the outside is fraught with obstacles, but if you start from the center, it's smooth sailing. You've got a bird's-eye view of every dead end. The clearest path of action becomes obvious. This is also the way to achieve your most important life goals, including finding love. *Start from your very center and work from there.* Your Core Gifts are your center.

Knowing your Core Gifts is like discovering a secret passageway to your capacity for love. In this chapter you'll learn more about Core Gifts and engage in a process of self-discovery that will lead you to identify two of your most essential Core Gifts.

YOUR CORE GIFTS

Your Core Gifts lie at the center of your new search for intimacy, because they are the deepest and most sensitive parts of you, the parts that feel love—and the effects of love—most intensely. Core

Gifts *come* from our core. They feel essential to our identity. To some degree Core Gifts are universal—for example, the desire to love and the need for a sense of self-determination. Yet our Core Gifts are also unique to us. If we look at our lives we find areas of particular sensitivity, vulnerability, and passion that are triggered by similar things. Something that hurts your feelings might roll off someone else's back; something that makes you feel deeply inspired may have little impact on someone else. We experience the most joy and the most pain around these highly charged parts of our being.

In your relationships you may be most prone to becoming angry or distant when you feel wounded around your Core Gifts. When you feel inspiration, validation, and acceptance around them, you'll shine. As we come to see the patterns of how we are affected by the experiences in our lives, our Core Gifts become clearer to us. Core Gifts aren't a gimmick, a packageable commodity that works like a genie to meet our deepest desires. They are the ache, the compelling pull, the inner *reaching* that we sometimes honor and sometimes try to silence. They are the music that keeps playing below the surface of our minds. To acknowledge our Core Gifts is to create deeper intimacy with our most essential self.

In physics, it is taught that the greater the mass of an object, the greater its gravity. Gravity is defined as a force that attracts other bodies to the center of the object. As you claim and honor your own Core Gifts, you will develop a more palpable sense of self, and this self holds the heft or the "mass" of your true identity. As you live from the weight of your real self, you'll develop more personal gravity. People who value gifts like yours will notice them and be drawn toward the center of *you*. You'll become more comfortable in your own skin. You will lose interest in relentless self-criticism, and you'll become a more generous person.

Why Are Our Core Gifts So Hard to Discover?

If our Core Gifts are at the very center of our identity, why are they so hard to recognize and so difficult to accept? The main reason is that most of them have rarely been called gifts or treated with the value a gift deserves. Maybe they've been labeled as oddness, over-sensitivity, or over-intensity, or maybe they've just never been seen as particularly special. Often our gifts are buried in our life story, and we miss their beauty and importance, despite those very gifts' having shaped our lives. But most of us have never been taught how to find those gifts, how to name them and nurture them. It's like learning a new language. Research shows that often we simply don't *see* things we don't have words for.[1]

Furthermore, our culture doesn't see the world in terms of gifts. Instead, we are taught to see life in terms of simple problems and solutions. We have not been taught that in order to understand our deepest suffering or our greatest joys, we must recognize the gifts that lie at their core. We have not been taught that honoring our vulnerability gives us a different kind of strength.

Often, our gifts are so basic to us that we may have never felt the need to single them out and name them—like a fish trying to grasp the concept of water. They are so basic to our inner life that it's hard for us to believe everyone doesn't have the same gifts. This can get us into a lot of trouble, because we expect everyone to hold the same values and sensitivities as we do, and when they don't meet the standards we set for ourselves—and don't even seem to care—we assume that it's because there's something wrong with us. Rather, it's simply a matter of realizing that our gifts are deeply unique, and that not everyone shares our sensitivities.

The Two Questions for Discovering Your Core Gifts

The easiest way to discover your gifts is to spend time thinking about these two questions:

- What hurts your heart the most?
- What fills your heart the most?

These questions are two of the greatest pathways to understanding the deeper story of our lives and our entire intimacy journey.

Knowing the answers to these questions will help you to cheat in the most lovely ways in the bewildering maze of dating. Remember, though: It is the work of a lifetime to understand your deep gifts. So enjoy every insight and every new understanding about your Core Gifts, without feeling that you must name and fully understand them. If they were that easy to identify, they would not be the hard-won treasures you'll find them to be.

FINDING YOUR CORE GIFTS IN YOUR JOYS

The quickest way to access your Core Gifts is by using the small moments of joy and meaning in your life as springboards. All of us, no matter how desperate our situation, experience moments when we feel nourished and inspired in our lives. We know when our heart feels particularly touched, when our spirit is quickened, when we feel loved, or when we are making a difference in someone's life. Moments when we truly *love* who we are.

We can use these experiences in two important ways to change our lives and speed our intimacy journey. First, when we open to these positive experiences more fully and stay with them just a bit longer than we might normally do, we actually develop our capacity for love. These moments are more than moments; they are actually portals, and the more we enter into them, the more our ability to love grows.

Second, when we pay attention to the experiences that fill our hearts, we discover what types of interactions and experiences inspire us and encourage us to open up and trust. When we take the time to notice these patterns, it's like a connect-the-dots game. What emerges is a picture of our Core Gifts.

In the target image, our Core Gifts lie in the center. Imagine these parts of yourself as a multifaceted gem. Every time you have a moment of connecting to your joy, it's as if a beam of light illuminates one facet of your Core Gifts. Each moment of joy is different and each moment illuminates a different facet of your nature. As time goes by you'll begin to develop greater familiarity with these different facets, and recognize your own sources of love and joy. In those moments there is a sense of truth, not necessarily a grand universal truth but a sense of personal truth, a feeling that says, "This touches me where I live." Such moments, easily passed over, are portals to our Core Gifts.

The World Craves Joy

The more you feel close to your joys, the more the people who are right for you will notice you and become attracted to you. Your joys are some of the very things your partner-to-be will love most about you, and will *need* most from you. Even in the course of this week as you do the exercises in this chapter, you'll notice positive changes in how you feel and in the quality of your interactions.

Also, the more time you spend with the things that touch you and move you, the more you will be noticed by the people who are good for you. *The kind of person you're seeking is someone who is drawn to your Core Gifts, your authentic self.* If you wait until you know someone loves you before you reveal these parts of yourself, it's as though you're waiting for the harvest without planting the seeds. It's the vulnerability, warmth, and humanity of your gifts that will make the right person notice and come to love you.

Pat, a dental hygienist, came to therapy because she was looking for love, but this time, she wanted *healthy* love. As she came to recognize her Core Gifts, she began to discover and embrace her deeper emotions. One of the places where those emotions hit her most intensely was in her dental office. She self-consciously admitted to me that when she worked on her patients, she often felt a sense of love and compassion for them that she feared could move her to tears. These feelings were so out of left field and so intense that she felt she had to suppress them in order to keep working. I suggested that these feelings came from the core of her authentic self, and that she should be grateful for them and try to enjoy them when they occurred. When she tried this, those feelings of love became deeper. She found that they would hit her at the oddest times: on the subway, seeing a child with his or her parents, sitting with her cat. They were a part of her, and when she gave herself permission to value them, she began to feel at home with these moments of streaming joy and compassion. By opening to these feelings, she felt she was coming to know her truest self. This completely changed her search for love. Now she knew this was the most precious part of her. If she couldn't touch and share this part of herself in an intimate relationship, that relationship wasn't worth having. Before she recognized this part of herself as a gift, she didn't really know its beauty or how important it would be to be able to share it in a relationship.

MICRO-MEDITATION
Someone You've Loved | Three minutes

Think about the person—or one of the people—you've loved most in your life. It can be anyone, even if that person is no longer alive—it just shouldn't be someone who broke your heart or was ultimately unavailable.

Picture the quality of this person's love for you. Remember a moment when you felt how much she or he cared about you.

What is the attribute you love most about this person? Describe how he or she has enriched your life. In your mind, find the words to thank this person. Feel the emotion ripples inside you. As you continue, feel that you are keeping this person in your heart.

In the next section of this chapter you will come to name two of your Core Gifts: one that you will find in the things that fill your heart and another that you will find in the things that hurt your heart. These processes are uplifting, but they are also challenging because they ask you to touch deep places inside. If you are not sure you're ready, or if you feel they might be destabilizing to you, please get support before trying them.

Discovering a Core Gift in Your Joys

Take some quiet, relaxed time with your journal for this very important process. Answer each question from the heart, feeling your feelings and not censoring what you write.

1. Recall and describe three times in your life when you felt most deeply inspired, "fed," or moved in a relationship with someone. Write a few sentences about each experience, describing what happened and what it felt like.

2. Read what you just wrote and allow yourself to savor each memory for a moment or two. Feel the ripples of emotion each one brings up. Now take a moment to reflect: Are there any common themes in these three experiences? What are they? What do these memories capture about you and about what inspires you in your relationships?

3. Choose the most important thing that these memories capture about you and about what inspires you in your relationships. Write one sentence to describe this important attribute of yourself.

4. How does it feel when this part of yourself is deprived of oxygen, squelched, or neglected in a relationship or in any part of your life? In one or two sentences, describe the pain you feel at those times.

5. Who in your life (past or present) helps this part of you to come alive and feel safe and welcomed? Pick two people with whom you have felt that way most strongly. Write their names, and a few words about how it feels to be with them

and to share this part of yourself. Then, take one moment to thank them silently.

6. Take another brief look at what you wrote, and appreciate the feelings that come with these memories. What's next shouldn't come as any surprise to you: the attribute you are describing is one of your Core Gifts! Remember, your Core Gifts live in the places where you care most.

Now name your Core Gift. Put words on it, even if they are imperfect words. In your journal, describe the worth of this Core Gift, its value to the world, its importance to you. Swing out. It may feel awkward to treasure this part of yourself, but the truth is that somewhere inside, you already do. It's just a matter of owning who you really are.

7. Take a moment to see if you can feel this Core Gift in you right now. If you can, that's wonderful. Enjoy it! If not, remember one of the memories you wrote about, and just imagine your Core Gift.

8. Is there a piece of music that captures or touches this part of you? If so, write down the title and replay it in your mind for a moment or two.

9. Is there an image in art or in nature that captures the spirit of this Core Gift? Write that down and allow yourself to feel it inside you.

10. If this gift had a message for your life, what would it be?

11. Take a moment to honor your Core Gift. Picture how your life will grow as you honor it more deeply and spend more time with the people who also know how to value it. Write a few sentences to describe your future as you learn to truly embrace and express this Core Gift in deeper ways.

Joy Makes Us Vulnerable

In doing this process you might find that you need to move away from the joy you may feel. This is normal. When we feel joy or pride in ourselves, most of us feel uncomfortable and try to minimize our good feelings. "Oh, well, everybody feels the same thing." Or we instantly parry our joy with a self-deprecating comment that degrades or minimizes the positive feeling we've just had. Joy is hard to bear. We shouldn't fool ourselves about that. And that's okay, we don't have to be able to bear it all at once. It's an almost homeopathic process. Drop by drop we learn to bear joy for longer and longer stretches of time. Carl Jung, a student of Freud and one of history's greatest psychoanalysts, says that all neurosis is a flight from authentic suffering. I think there's great truth to this. But I also think that much neurosis is a flight from authentic joy.

One of our greatest life tasks is actually to learn to bear joy, and to let it influence our psychology in deeper and deeper ways. In actuality, there is a great cultural discomfort with joy, and our voracious pleasure seeking is often a mask for our fear of simple joy. Joy frightens us, it makes our defenses quake — it almost invites a superstitious fear of "the other shoe dropping." We can bear joy for fleeting moments, but for most of us, self-appreciation all too quickly devolves into self-measurement.

In my work as a therapist I watch for these moments of inspiration and try not to let them pass. I encourage my clients to stay with their inspiring moment just a bit longer. When they do, something surprisingly deep will likely emerge. Kevin, a client who did this process with me, said, "I never put this into words, but now I know how I survived all that I've been through. I have a rock of joy inside me, and it never really leaves me. I never really knew it until this moment."

You have similar gifts inside you, and the more you savor your small moments of inspiration, the better you will come to know them — and be changed by them.

I suggest that you stop now, and allow these insights to filter through you for at least a few hours before you move on to the next part. You've just done some very profound work.

OUR CORE GIFTS AND OUR WOUNDS

We experience not only the greatest joy but the greatest pain around our Core Gifts because we feel intuitively that our identity rests there. How could it be otherwise? These gifts hold our greatest yearning, our compassion for others, our broken parts, and our most profound needs.

The very qualities that we are most ashamed of, the places where we have been most hurt and feel most insecure, all reflect our Core Gifts, and hence have the power to point the way to real love. The places where our heart has been broken reflect how deep our bonds can go. The things that hurt us most reflect the places where we are still innocent, still tender. These tender parts of us lie at the very core of our ability to find love. When anything makes us feel compassion and care—even if the feeling carries heartache—we are in our Gift Zone. Our hurting heart is the part that cares most about love.

I see this in my son, who becomes highly attached to the things and beings in his world. We had a loving and wonderful cat named Katherine when he was young. He was deeply attached to her. She passed away when he was about six, and his grief was profound. Even a year after her death, he would sometimes sit with a blanket draped over his head and body, stroking a picture of our cat that he had drawn, tears dripping onto the picture. I wondered and I worried: Was this a problem? Was he stuck in something unhealthy or morbid? But I came to realize that this was a sign of the depth of his ability to connect. I said to him, "This pain comes from your gift, because it shows how very deeply you love. And as you grow older and you find your own loves in your life, this is how fully you're going to love them. This gift means that you're going to have a life that is full of love, because this is how deep your heart is."

If I had shamed him for the depth of his caring, he would have had to create armor around that gift. If I hadn't coached him in how to honor the almost unbearable burden of his gift, he would have felt ashamed of the depth of his love. Now, he could at least honor himself as he grieved, and that honoring helped him find his own path to healing.

One night, long after Katherine died, he was crying in my arms; once again, his tears weren't stopping. "Okay," I said, "we need to go to the beach." We packed up and walked to the boardwalk, and he lay there, looking up at the stars, softly crying. Something happened then. He said, "Dad, I feel her. I feel Katherine. I feel her here." And his tears stopped. We stayed for a while on that bench, and finally we walked home together. That night marked the end of his relentlessly haunting grief.

Why do we incur pain around such profound and wonderful parts of ourselves? Following are four of the most important reasons why this happens. As you read this next section, notice which of these experiences you identify with.

First, people take advantage of others' gifts, often without even realizing they are doing it. Caregivers who have their own wounds often "milk" their children's talents and gifts, or they might ignore, neglect, or even disdain these gifts. For example, a lonely parent might exploit a child's gift of empathy, using the child as a confidant concerning intimate adult issues, and at another point might shame the child for being "oversensitive." After being used in such a way, we become wary of the intentions of those close to us.

Second, we are most tender and vulnerable in the places we care the most, so we have the potential of being most hurt in these places. You will be more sensitive than most people around your Core Gifts. *In fact, one of the ways you know you're touching a Core Gift is that you've repeatedly been told "You're too sensitive" around it.* In all probability, people do experience you as too sensitive around your Core Gifts, because they don't have the exquisite antennae that you have. You may notice things in your environment and in the interactions around you that other people are completely unaware of.

When we express these parts of our soul to someone who doesn't "get it" or who takes advantage of us, it's humiliating. Something inside us cringes. We begin to think, *Is there something wrong with me for this quality?* In fact, that's another way we can recognize our Core Gifts. We've been embarrassed by them.

These parts of us are also most at risk of being abused. And abuse creates a surgical bond between pain and our most precious gifts. After abuse, it becomes hard to experience the gift without re-experiencing the pain associated with it. As a result, we often feel weakest around these sensitive parts of ourselves. Yet those "weak" places are connected to our greatest gifts, whether we know it or not.

Third, our gifts are rarely just simple and sweet! They are profound, and they can demand a great deal of us and those around us. They are often challenging and sometimes threatening to others. They lead us to the points of greatest truth, creativity, and freedom, but those are not always easy things to experience. They can give us the greatest joy imaginable, but they never stop challenging us to join them in deeper and deeper places. We may have been frightened by the differentness, passion, and vulnerability of these places.

Our Core Gifts have their roots in a land of feeling and perception that is greater than this one. We can honor them, but we can never fully tame them; nor should we be able to. Genius domesticated is genius lost. In order to grow and develop our gifts, we need to honor their fire, even if that fire scares and challenges us.

Fourth, we've messed up, and had "car crashes" around our gifts. In fact, our deepest immaturities and greatest points of dysfunction usually surround these gifts. It is our life's work to learn to bear these gifts, and without that hard work, we will keep making the same two basic mistakes around our Core Gifts: suppressing them or acting out in connection with them. Acting out means expressing them in ways that are harmful to ourselves and others. Whenever a gift hasn't had a chance to grow up, there will be a lack of grace in the way we express it, usually shown in behavior that is overly aggressive or unnecessarily timid.

If you recognize any of these dynamics in yourself, you have found a point of deep sensitivity. Your sensitivity is an attribute of your greatest self, no matter how much pain it has caused you. Sensing what is happening in our heart, in our environment, and in the hearts of others is a profound gift. In fact, a well-known Buddhist teacher named Jigme Khyentse Rinpoche calls our Buddha nature (our state of natural divinity) a state of "unbearable tenderness."[2] My guess, if you've come this far with me, is that you relate to these words. Have you ever felt a sense of unbearable tenderness?

Susan came to therapy after her boyfriend of two years left her. She had put the whole of her heart and all her energies into her relationship, and when it ended, she felt utterly destroyed. On her first visit she asked me, "Why can't I let go and move on like he did or like my friends tell me I should? Why do I hurt so much more than other people from these things?"

As she began to tell me the stories of her life, I could see a powerful pattern emerging again and again: I saw how softhearted and kind she was — and how most of her loved ones relied on these qualities but never fully honored them or reciprocated her generosity. Her friends and family couldn't really understand the devastation that her breakup caused her. People were so busy. No one had the same kind of time for her that she would have had for them.

Her ex-boyfriends had always appreciated the gift of her generosity, but on some level, none of them ever really got it. And when her relationships ended, she was hurt not only by the loss but also by the feeling of not being understood, of not being seen, and of being taken advantage of. "Why am I brought down by my caring?" she asked. "And why do I keep dating guys who hurt me?"

Susan sometimes felt that her generosity and tenderness were a curse. I suggested that those qualities were a gift and I sensed that a key to her healing lay precisely there. I asked her to describe these qualities as if they were a gift. She described, "a bone-deep capacity to put love first, an innate generosity, sensitivity, and kindness."

It sounds simple, but just labeling these qualities as a gift was the foundation of a new future for her. By seeing their worth she could learn to understand, honor, and even treasure them—and to recognize when those around her could not. She began to blame herself less for other people's insensitivity.

She spoke about friends who would drop the ball after she had been there for them, about boyfriends who gradually took more and more advantage of her. She realized that on some level she was taught to be ashamed of her generosity and openness, and that eventually translated into self-hate. That's what made her feel weak. That's what ultimately left her devastated when her boyfriends broke up with her. She also noticed that most of the close relationships in her life, from childhood on, had these same dynamics. We discussed how these abuses hit her in the places she cared about the most, that her worst pain came when her generosity was misunderstood or her sensitivity was trampled on.

Somewhere inside, Susan always knew the value of her kindness, but she hated that it left her with a feeling of weakness. She worked on learning to love her gift and on acknowledging how rare it was. She practiced looking at her life through that filter, and it became instantly clear who treasured her gift and who didn't. In time she told me that she felt like a warrior.

Susan finally felt she had the right to protect her tender heart. I watched as her inner beauty grew, along with her sense of worth. She stopped spending so much time trying to win over those who didn't get her and she learned to lean on those who did. These true friends kept reminding her of what she was doing whenever she fell back into the pattern of feeling responsible for others' insensitivity.

When Susan looked at her life through the lens of her gift, she felt triumphant: "I was right all along! Those things that bothered me about my boyfriends bothered me for a reason. I wasn't crazy. I just didn't fully honor my gift, and I found men who were all too happy to agree."

As Susan learned to honor her gift, her life began to change. When faced with unkindness, she didn't immediately blame herself. I watched as she began to develop a fierce protective wisdom around her gift. She remained kind and was able to give to the people around her in many new ways. But now her radar was working, and she knew how to distinguish kindness from unkindness. She realized that when people subtly or harshly demeaned her tenderness, it felt very familiar and it brought up her old feelings of deep inadequacy. No one had ever taught her she had a gift that needed to be honored, cared for, and helped to become strong in the world. She found that she was taking stock of all her relationships in a new way. There were the friends and family who were kind to her, and there were those who cut at her. There were the friends who needed lots of support but wouldn't give the same back, and there were the ones who gave as generously as she did. They were the people she needed to be with in order to have a happy life. Because of her gift, she didn't have the "luxury" of spending unnecessary time with people who were callous or selfish. This change brought about a shift in her entire dating life. Although she remained "sticky" to people who switched between being kind and abusive, she found that she had lost her tolerance for abuse. If someone she was seeing was hurtful, she would explain how she felt, and if he treated her badly in the same way again, she would simply move on. Soon she was dating men who inspired her with their kindness and the creativity with which they lived their lives.

The Essential Art of Discrimination

Our tears are a great gift because they reveal what matters most to us. Understanding the pains that were once wordless and knotted within us—and then putting an explanation on them—is life changing.

How many times have you sensed something "off" in a relationship, and told yourself that you were being oversensitive, only to find later that you were right on target? Usually when we sense something is off, it's because something *is* off! Our interpretation of exactly what is "off" may be askew, but our sense that something isn't right is usually accurate and is always worthy of being listened to. Often we flee our discomfort before honoring its wisdom.

Our task in the intimacy journey is to find relationships that essentially feel right in the ways that matter most. To recognize what feels right, we need to know what feels *wrong*—and how to say no to it. In the course of your relationships and your day-to-day interactions, you will learn much about your path to intimacy simply by noticing what feels right and what feels wrong.

When something feels wrong to us and we haven't yet developed the ability to handle it skillfully, we usually react in one or both of the two ways previously described: suppression or acting out. Suppressing our pain or anger weakens us. Acting out hurts us and others. When we learn to listen to our own sensitivities about what feels wrong to us we become empowered. Then we can speak about the things that feel wrong in an appropriate way, honoring our feelings and the feelings of others who may be triggering the pain. However, we must learn to discern who deserves the treasure of our vulnerability. Are we sharing a tender sensitivity with someone who keeps hurting us? That is not something we want to do. Are we sharing with someone who has proved himself to be caring and honoring of who we are? In those cases it may be wise to share our feelings. As we learn to honor our sensitivities, our defenses slowly transform into skills and we strengthen our ability to be in an intimate relationship.

Michael, a highly accomplished professional, came to therapy to work on a number of issues, including his anger. At an early point in his therapy, he told me that he was afraid to be in a serious romantic relationship out of fear that his anger could do emotional damage to his future partner.

During one session he told me a story that helped us reframe his anger as a gift. He was in a third world country and he befriended a young girl who sold postcards next to a monument. Day after day, he would buy new cards and chat with her. He loved her childlike enthusiasm, her intelligence, and her feisty nature. In time he noticed that a local policeman would take some of her money each day. One day, the little girl fought back and told him she wasn't giving her money to him. Michael watched this interaction and tried to stay out of it—until the policeman began to beat her. That was all he could take. He flung himself on the policeman, slammed him into a fence, pinned his arm behind his back, and screamed at the little girl to get away. The child escaped and somehow, so did Michael. It was only later that he realized how much danger he had put himself in.

In light of this and other stories Michael told me, we realized that all his episodes of rage were attempts to fight against unfairness, usually toward others. He had come from a brutal background, but he never became brutal unless someone was being hurt or treated unfairly. He had always been aware of the destructiveness of his rage, but he had never been able to see the heroism, the fierce protectiveness, at its core. Michael learned to see his rage not as a pathology that had to be cured but as a powerful gift that had to be channeled. His gift was like a wild horse. He couldn't get the reins until he honored its beauty and power.

Discovering a Core Gift through Your Tears

Take some quiet, relaxed time with your journal for this very important process. Answer each question from the heart, honoring your feelings and not censoring what you write.

1. Think about a tender and important part of you that has not been honored in more than one of your relationships. Remember two times you have felt hurt, misunderstood, ignored, abused, or taken advantage of around this particular part of you. Describe each experience in a few short sentences. If possible have at least one of your examples be from a romantic relationship.

2. Look at what you wrote. If this is a tender part of you where you have felt hurt more than a few times in your life, you are likely touching a Core Gift. Put words on the particular hurt that you feel when this part of you is not honored. Feel the familiarity of that pain. It is a part of your journey, and the more you feel its familiarity, the more empowered you will become to free yourself of it.

3. Now, think about someone in your life who has been able to appreciate this vulnerable part of you. Name this person and describe how it feels when this part of you feels appreciated, safe, and free.

4. Take a moment to internally thank this person, describing what you appreciate about him or her. By doing this you strengthen your own connection to that person and to your Core Gift.

5. Name your Core Gift that lies in the heart of these past hurts. Naming it as a gift and not as a flaw is a powerful act of self-love. Let me give you a few suggestions to help you do this:

You may think, *This is not a gift—it's a curse.* In fact, those exact words are one of the greatest markers of a profound gift. Our Core Gifts often feel like curses until we learn how to handle their power and sensitivity.

You may not want to call it a gift because you are ashamed of some of the things it has made you do. That's another sign of a gift. When we act out or suppress a part of ourselves, that it is a marker of a gift we haven't learned to honor.

Try to let go of your old viewpoint as you learn this new understanding of the meaning of gifts. Describe this characteristic as a gift, not a weakness, even if it's hard to do so. I promise you, you will find a gift there. Put words on it, even if they are imperfect words. If you still feel stuck, picture the person you just wrote about who values this part of you. How would he or she describe it as a gift?

If you are still having a difficult time naming your Core Gift, here are some examples of other peoples' descriptions of their Core Gift:

- I am deeply loyal and can't comprehend how people can leave someone they love.

- I am empathic. I feel the pain of other people around me and their pain causes me to hurt.

- I sense when things are wrong or unspoken in relationships, even when others don't seem to notice.

- I care deeply about truth, and I speak honestly even when other people are afraid to.

- I go out of my way to help others.

- I am generous and it gives me joy to give to others, even though many people have taken advantage of that generosity.

Now, write one or two sentences that identify the Core Gift you have found in your tears.

6. Think about how you feel when your gift is cherished and honored instead of degraded or hurt. Let an image come that captures that feeling and write it down. Imagine what your life would be like as you learn to honor this gift and surround yourself with people who also honor it, as you honor theirs.

I encourage you to make a promise to yourself. Do not continue to date anyone, anymore, *ever*, who doesn't value this gift of yours in a basic and consistent way. And when you date someone who does value that part of you, let yourself learn to become accustomed to the new and perhaps foreign sense of safety and happiness you may feel.

HONORING OUR GIFTS

Whenever you feel a Core Gift inside you, take an extra beat to stay with your experience. When you do, it's very likely you will have a small swell of warmth inside you. That moment is gold. Let that swell move through you and then pass. You don't have to do anything more. Appreciating the feeling will deepen you and allow that same gift to come up more frequently. Love of self and love of another begin with the honoring of our Core Gifts.

Only by connecting with our Core Gifts can we ever hope to transcend our wounds and our "unworthiness." Because somehow, even as we get closer to our demons, each layer inward makes us feel more certain of who we are and what we are meant to do in the world. Each layer inward brings us to another level of passion. Each layer inward allows us to love more deeply, and each trains us in a new level of skill, bravery, and wisdom.

Because we have suffered deep wounds, most of us have closed parts of ourselves off to our Core Gifts. When our gifts are misunderstood, a part of our heart breaks. So we toughen up and think, *I'm never going to make it in the world if I show these parts of myself.* We tuck those parts of ourselves away and lock them up, even from ourselves.

Susan wouldn't let her partners know that she needed the same kind of nurturing she was giving to them. She didn't realize that by ignoring her gifts, she was committing an act of quiet violence against herself, a violence that always led to some form of harm in her relationships.

I have found that the wisest way to get a handle on our gifts is to allow ourselves to stand back a bit and feel a sense of awe for them. I have practiced this many times with my clients as they have revealed the depth of their love, their need, their tenderness, and their hurt. In those moments, I feel more like a witness than anything else. Imagine standing in front of the vastness of the Grand Canyon. You can't cross it. You can't enlarge it or shrink it.

You can't own or control it. But you can stand on the edge of its vastness and feel awe. Awe disappears when we chip away at ourselves for our imperfections. It returns when we name our gifts and recognize their humanity. When you can think about any gift and feel a sense of awe, then your gift has the power to reach you, to change you.

To understand one's deepest wounds and challenges, one needs to ask this question: "What is the Core Gift that is trying to express itself at the heart of this struggle?" Sometimes the answer can't be reduced to a word or a phrase. And we often need the insight of others to help us decipher our Core Gifts. Creating a relationship with our Core Gifts is the task of a lifetime. Most of us must practice exposing ourselves to our Core Gifts in small doses, gradually increasing our tolerance for their power, their tenderness — and their immense challenge. Our deepest gifts can grow and mature, but they can never be domesticated. They will never fit into the small, safe, well-mannered boxes we create for them. They will continue to draw outside the lines, to get us in trouble, cajole us to the edge of authenticity, cause tears we don't understand, surprise us with their emotion-filled truths.

We spend so much time trying to get our gifts to listen to us, to line up in a nice row, to do what we tell them. Guess who loses that battle time and time again? Until we cherish the gift at the heart of our flaws, we will forever live in knots. More important, we will miss out on the magic that makes us who we are, and that allows the precious people who are made for us to finally discover *where* we are.

To ignore your Core Gifts is to commit an act of quiet violence against yourself. My hope is that you can allow yourself an answer-less awe at their mystery and their humanity.

In this chapter, you have begun the process of discovering your own Core Gifts. This rich and invaluable process continues in the workbook exercises, which will take you on a fascinating journey of self-discovery around your gifts. These exercises are an essential part of this stage. They will help you gain a deeper sense of the hidden genius of your Core Gifts.

Deeper Dating Workbook

PERSONAL EXERCISES

Finding Your Gifts through Your Joys and Your Tears

Do parts A and B of this exercise together over the course of two days. In that time you'll learn a huge amount about the Core Gifts that have always lived within you, and you'll develop a much deeper appreciation of the "genius" in your unique sensitivities. Do not skip these exercises. They have the power to help you build a self-loving foundation for the rest of your intimacy journey.

A. Finding Your Gifts through Inspiration

Over a period of two days, notice which interactions with others bring you joy, or touch or inspire you. Each day, answer these questions for one of these inspiring interactions:

- What was the interaction?

- What was the good feeling it gave you? (Describe that feeling.)

- What gift of yours was validated or nourished in this interaction? Put words on that gift—even if it feels egotistical or awkward!

- What does this say about the other person and your relationship?

B. Finding Your Gifts through Your Hurts

Over a period of two days, notice which of your interactions cause a sense of hurt (even minor hurt) that somehow feels *familiar* to you. Answer these questions for one hurtful interaction each day. Most of us tend to allow ourselves to be hurt in the same ways again and again. *When this occurs, there's a Core Gift below that pattern that we have not learned to honor.* Answer the following questions.

And remember: When you try to articulate the gift beneath the pain, don't look for strength. Don't look for talent or skill. Just look for the beating heart of your humanity. That's a sure sign that a Core Gift is lying right beneath. Now answer the following questions:

- What was the interaction?

- What was the pain or discomfort it gave you?

- How does it remind you of other kinds of wounds you've had in the past?

- Identify and describe the Core Gift that was hurt in this interaction. (Perhaps for the first time, allow yourself to honor the deep sensitivity of your gift. Don't simply say, "What's wrong with me for being so sensitive?")

- Consider whether this interaction points to a problem in your relationship with the other person. If so, how do you understand that problem? Can you address it in a loving way that is safe for you and the other person?

After doing these exercises for two days, take some time to reflect on what you wrote. Then answer these questions:

1. What have you learned about yourself and your Core Gifts? Does this help to explain any of the joys and heartbreaks in your past close relationships?

2. Go back to your definition of the Core Gift you found in your joys and the one you found in your tears. Do you have any further insights about these gifts?

LEARNING PARTNER EXERCISE
Name Your Core Gifts

Share your reflections about this chapter's work with your learning partner. If you got stuck in naming your gifts, let your partner help you. Go over your answers to each of the exercises you've done both in the body of the chapter and in the workbook section. Work with your partner to help deepen both of your understandings of your Core Gifts.

3

How to Love Yourself First

It is an absolute human certainty that no one can know his own beauty or . . . worth until it has been reflected back to him in the mirror of another loving, caring human being.

—JOHN JOSEPH POWELL, *The Secret of Staying in Love*

As you begin to glimpse the promise that lies in your gifts you are probably also seeing how challenging they can be. Once you embrace your Core Gifts, they begin to take on a life of their own. They ask you to drop your patterns of self-protection and disconnection and to learn new and more authentic ways of being in the world. They can't bear to be squashed or demeaned. They yearn for new levels of communication, sexual intimacy, laughter, and adventure. As you allow yourself to embrace and reveal these more authentic, vulnerable parts of yourself, you come upon a new challenge: How can you protect yourself as you express your authenticity more bravely and fully in your dating life?

FROM DEFENSES TO SKILLS

Many dating books focus on teaching us how to strengthen and polish our protective armor. This book teaches us a way to honor our most tender self beneath the armor and still remain strong, brave, and true to who we are. With this approach comes the acknowledgment and the recognition of the sensitivity we may have around our gifts, and the development of new skills to protect those gifts.

In nature, creatures are endowed with either exoskeletons or endoskeletons. Those with exoskeletons protect their soft parts with a hard outer armor. Creatures with endoskeletons have bodies that are formed around the solid but flexible inner structure of their skeleton. Their soft parts can be exposed because of the integrity of their inner framework. When we embrace who we really are and begin to accept our limitations, we feel we have an endoskeleton, or a spine, and we become secure in our trust of its presence. We can meet the world skin to skin. When we are ashamed of who we are or don't have the skills we need to protect ourselves, there's only one option: hiding behind a brittle armor of defenses that keeps the world at a distance. When the world feels unsafe—and particularly when we haven't learned, or been taught, to honor our gifts—we rely on our hardened, habitual defenses to protect these tender parts of our being.

All of us build different kinds of armor to protect ourselves. The types of defenses we create are as varied as our personalities. Some of us may use humor to keep the world at bay. Some use anger. Some use people-pleasing. These defenses wrap around our gifts and wounds and don't let anything risky inside. In their more extreme (or "primitive") forms, these defenses are black and white. They are overreactive and habitual, and we bring them to almost every relationship we enter. Ultimately, they don't work.

There is a formula that governs the architecture of our whole intimacy lives: to the degree that we neglect our gifts, we are actually committing an act of quiet violence against ourselves. By dishonoring our gifts, we create a vacuum within our being, in the very place where our gifts should reside. Nature abhors a vacuum. Therefore, that vacuum becomes filled with unhealthy relationships, or with our own self-sabotage or pain. After decades as a psychotherapist—and a lifetime of being me—I am still in awe of the power of this dynamic. I've never seen it not be true.

Therefore, as we learn to live from our center, or our gifts, we need to evolve past the brittle and self-limiting defenses we relied on in the past.

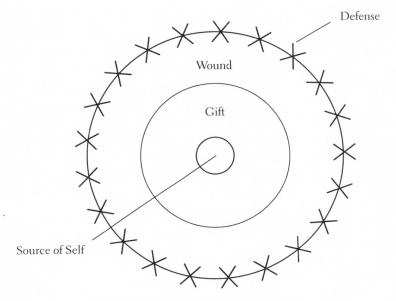

Diagram 2: The Gift-Wound-Defense Matrix

Wiser Self-Protection

Our defenses may hurt us and those around us, and they may hold us back from our potential, but they were forged out of the worthy goal of self-protection. As we commit to expressing our Core Gifts, we are faced with an important task: we must learn to outgrow our prepackaged defenses and interact skin to skin with the world. We can begin to do that by finding the gifts that lie beneath our defenses and wounds.

Here is a way to understand your entire intimacy journey. I call it the Gift-Wound-Defense Matrix (see diagram 2):

- At the heart of every defense lies a wound.

- At the heart of every wound lies a gift.

- At the heart of every gift lies a portal to the Source of Self—the key to our deepest love and life-meaning.

Because our defenses, our wounds, and our gifts are all part of the same matrix, we can use each one as an entry point to understand the others. Our gifts reveal our wounds; our defenses reveal our gifts. They are all part of the same whole.

Let's come back to Lisa from chapter 1 to illustrate our diagram of the Gift-Wound-Defense Matrix. When Lisa's boyfriend was fixating on the remote instead of connecting with her, she started to get angry. In the past she would have become defensive, acting out her anger by getting prickly and putting up a wall against her boyfriend—all the while being angry at herself for being so oversensitive. Those behaviors were her defenses. As we have seen, beneath every defense lies a wound. Lisa's wound was her feeling of insecurity and separation because she was longing for closeness with her boyfriend—and she was worried that he didn't feel the same. Lisa also suffered from an even deeper wound: a sense of shame around her deep need for connection and affirmation. Diagram 2 shows that beneath every wound lies a gift. That night, after using the intimacy-fix exercise, Lisa got to experience her gift—a deep need for closeness and an ability to lean into love. By asking for what she needed in a caring way, she discovered how safe her boyfriend was for her—he didn't deride, criticize, or ignore her—in fact, he put the remote down, curled up with her, listened to her feelings, and told her that he also really cared about her. In the happiness Lisa felt at that moment, she experienced an inner "rightness" both with herself and with her boyfriend. In that experience, she opened a portal to a sense of deeper love and meaning in her own life—a connection to her Source of Self.

As Lisa discovered that night, our true protection doesn't come from layering on the armor. It comes from honoring our gift, and then doing the best we can to choose someone who is kind, giving, and accepting of who we are. Whenever you feel your defenses taking over, you can use this model to discover the wound you're protecting, the gift beneath that wound, and the deeper sense of love and meaning your gift can offer you.

Finding Your Gift through Your Defenses

Let's take a moment to do an exciting piece of self-discovery that will make this idea come alive for you—and open up your search for love in a wonderful way. See what happens as you try this short but very potent thought exercise:

1. What is a part of your personality that you suppress or feel hesitant or timid to reveal in your romantic life?

2. How do you behave in order to suppress this part of your personality? (*This is your defense.*)

3. How have you been hurt or unappreciated in relation to this part of yourself? (*This is your wound.*)

4. Who has respected and appreciated this part of you?

5. How do you feel when you are with someone like this?

6. In one or two sentences, describe this part of you as a gift. Describe its worth, its value, and its potential. It may feel like a stretch, but it will open doors for you to do so. (*This is your gift.*)

7. If you honored and expressed this part of you with increasing generosity and wisdom, how might it lead you to deeper love and meaning in your life? (*This is your portal to your Source of Self.*)

In most cases, the quality we feel most timid about revealing in our romantic or dating life is in reality one of our most central and defining gifts. If you can begin to honor this part of yourself—reveal it more, and stick with those precious people who know how to value it—your dating life and your entire intimacy life will change in ways you can't yet imagine. Can you picture allowing this gift to unfold, and being with someone who truly values it?

That is one of your foundations for love that can last—and that man or woman is out there right now, waiting for someone like you. This quality in you has been part of the missing link in your search for love. Learn to treasure it, and I promise you, your life will unfold in remarkable ways.

THE SECRET TO SELF-WORTH

The feeling that our gifts are unworthy is like an old and painful hypnosis. There are two pathways to break free from that hypnosis. First, by seeing these attributes as gifts and building a loving relationship with them, we gradually become free from the painful thrall of that hypnosis. Second, by finding our "tribe," the people who honor and value us for who we are, we open our life up to true happiness. Both are necessary steps to loving ourselves—and to finding love.

Developing Our Relationship with Our Gifts

Our Core Gifts are our children. They are born from within us. They must be fed by us if they are to flourish. They depend upon us because we are the broker between them and the world. Our choices rule their existence. They can rebel. They can act up. They can shut down. But they can't help us make decisions for our lives unless we give them a place at the voting table. We may not always like what they decide, or what they have to say. In fact, just like any good parent we must submit ourselves to be turned completely inside out by the needs of our children, facing our blind spots and our weak spots simply because we have to, because we love them so much.

Enjoying Our Gifts

In his book *The Childhood Roots of Adult Happiness*, Dr. Edward Hallowell teaches that one of the most important things we can do to ensure that our children will grow into happy adults is that we simply *enjoy* them.[1] More than anything else, this instills in them the deep belief that they are pleasurable, cherished, worthy. Simply enjoying them is perhaps the greatest determinant of our children's future happiness. And it's the same with our gifts. Are we enjoying our gifts? Are we playing with them and delighting in them? Are we looking at them and relishing the possibilities they bring into our lives? That's how they become happy, powerful, and secure.

Our gifts need what every child needs: quality time with us. A current relationship filled with honesty and authenticity. Authentic dialogue between them and us so that they are finally able to breathe, to have oxygen in this world. Unlike our children, though, we will always be the primary relationship for our gifts. No one else can serve that role. The world can be difficult, bullying, and unkind, but if our gifts know they have us as protectors, there's a profound sense of safety that allows them freedom.

Encouraging Our Gifts

Hallowell says that another way to ensure that our children become happy adults is to teach them mastery. Mastery over their fears. A belief that they can get through obstacles and over hurdles. Our Core Gifts long to be respected enough to be developed. They hunger to test themselves, to push past fears, obstacles, and "obstacle illusions." They want independence, creative freedom, and expression.

A gifted child hungers to have her gifts seen and acknowledged. Our gifts hunger for a mentor who honors them, delights in their flights of excess, shelters their vulnerability, and then sends them out into the world to take risks. Our gifts aren't stagnant. They long to take us somewhere. They compel us to take a risk, to turn the next corner, meet the next challenge, to devour our next limitation.

When we learn to call them "gifts" instead of imperfections, they find freedom from our crippling cautiousness. That's when they become joyously, ferociously hungry for the next new learning. And that's when life becomes truly exciting. Without our backing, our gifts are like children who are afraid to try. It's our job as their parents to *encourage* them to try. In your search for love, "trying" means sharing your authentic self and reaching out to the rare and precious people who can honor these parts of you.

Sharing Our Gifts

Our gifts also need to know that people need them. They hunger to give to the world and be received, because unfettered giving is one of life's absolute joys. Your Core Gifts must be given, must be shared, and must touch others. And you must see this happening before you can ever feel that your gifts—and by extension, you—are truly worthy.

In my many years of practice as a psychotherapist, I have seen something very important: it is those clients who have a generosity of spirit who are capable of finding the greatest happiness. They are also most resilient in the face of trauma and disaster. If they are also wise enough to choose relationships in which their generosity is appreciated and returned, their lives become profoundly gratifying.

When you're getting to know someone new, if you quash your generosity you will feel somehow reduced. If you don't seize the moment and take your date's hand when you feel like it, something is lost. Saying "I love you" and touching your partner sexually or sensually in a way that speaks from your deepest heart are both acts of generosity. And the experience of having someone respond with joy and reciprocation provides a deep sense of mastery for your gifts. "I can live in this world," they begin to say. "I can be powerful. I can be generous. I am wanted. I can love."

Cultivating Our Gifts' Complements

Our gifts must have a strong foundation in the world. Paradoxically, for this to happen we must develop their complementary quality within us: Our vulnerability needs bravery in order to be shared in the world. The visionary needs practicality in order for her creations to come to life. The practical person needs to cultivate his dreamer-self in order to create beauty in his life. The generous person must learn to say no.

To be sure, it's an uphill battle to cultivate the opposite quality of your dominant gifts. On some level, most of us would just rather not do the work. But when we do it, something great happens. We find our self-respect growing. We feel more solid, more self-confident, more in control.

In your search for love, bear in mind this fascinating insight: the less we have cultivated the qualities that are opposite to our gifts, the more we will be attracted to people who carry that complementary quality in a negative way. For example, a person who is generous of spirit but can't set limits will tend to be attracted to someone who is great at taking but not good at giving back. The more we cultivate these complementary qualities within ourselves, the more we'll find ourselves attracted to people who appreciate our gifts, and who won't take advantage of us.

Honoring the Cost of Our Gifts

Each of our gifts carries its own costs, and those costs are real. Someone who has a deep sense of loyalty usually has known the great pain of staying too long in a relationship that doesn't serve him or her. Someone who sees through hypocrisy and can't bear dishonesty knows the pain of being punished for speaking the truth. People with humility know the pain of being unseen. And people who bond deeply know the pain of separation in the keenest ways.

As we learn to understand and honor our gifts, we can lessen the pain these gifts carry in their wake. The more skilled we are at using our gifts in wise ways—and this is the work of a lifetime—the less burdensome they become. But to some degree, part of the wise stewardship of a gift is to accept the pain that comes with it. It is the price of the greatness within us. It is the cost of being human, of having a soul. Many of us flee our gifts because we dread paying the price of them. To become mature means learning to own and honor the cost of our gifts in this world.

Think of one of your Core Gifts. Think of the cost of this gift in your life. Take a moment to recognize that you cared so much that you paid that cost, whether wisely or unwisely.

As you learn to honor that gift and respect the cost it carries, you will be much less likely to squander it on people and situations that cannot honor it.

Our Gifts Hunger for Their Own Greatness

Our Core Gifts also hunger for greatness. But just as we have rethought the meaning of gifts, so too can we rethink the meaning of greatness.

Greatness is not fame or success. It is something much more humbling, and much more challenging. As we feed the hungers of our Core Gifts, we find ourselves touching the hem of some kind of greatness, one that might not even have words. We sense that we are closer to some unnamed native land that we may have never seen but have still been homesick for our entire lives.

Our society's love of fame is a cheapened expression of this hunger for personal greatness. Sometimes, when I'm cooking in the kitchen, chatting with a loved one, I feel my heart leap with a happiness that is almost painfully sharp but endlessly simple. That's greatness to me.

Our Gifts Need Us to Discriminate

There's no way around the fact that we are truly taking a risk when we share the most vulnerable parts of ourselves. That is why we must remember that the more we reveal our vulnerability, our tenderness, our heart, and our soul, the more we must exercise our powers of discrimination by saying no to situations and people that don't feed or support us. In chapter 2 I wrote about the art of discrimination. Now, let's take that concept a bit further.

Often, especially if we are trying to grow, be kind, or be spiritual in our relationships, we suppress our sense of what's wrong, telling ourselves we should spend more time cultivating gratitude and less time being so "negative." Cultivating gratitude is one of the greatest things we can do for ourselves, but we must also learn to honor our feelings of nongratitude—like a gut-level sense that something's wrong. These troubling feelings hold half the key for achieving our most precious life goals. In our quest for love we must mature past the dehumanizing belief that any time we're not grateful, we're being negative. Ignoring our innate sense of discrimination leads to debilitating self-doubt, not enlightenment. Often, the opposite of gratitude is not ingratitude — it's discrimination.

Countless times I've seen people keep trying to convince themselves to be more accepting, more patient, more disciplined — to be the bigger person—when their gut-level discomfort is dead-on accurate. I've watched so many loved ones and clients stay too long in unhealthy relationships, just because they thought they weren't strong enough, grateful enough, or disciplined enough to fix things.

Michael Clemente, a brilliant performer who died of AIDS in the early 1990s and one of the closest friends I've ever had, once announced that he found a way to "get blood from a stone," and was going to teach his audience his tried-and-true method, perfected through years of relationships with emotionally unavailable partners. "Take a rock and just keep hitting yourself in the head with it," he said. "After a while, you'll become so disoriented that you won't know if the blood is coming from you or from the stone!" This painful image captures what we do to ourselves when we try too hard to ignore our very real discomfort in certain relationships and life situations.

At the risk of oversimplification (and excluding cases of active addiction and untreated psychological disorders), we feel good when important things feel right in our lives. We register that "rightness" with feelings of peace, gratification, and stability. These are signs that our Core Gifts, those barometers of our very soul, are being honored, seen, and embraced. When things feel wrong, we feel empty, sad, hurting. These are signs that our Core Gifts are somehow not being seen or honored — by others, and quite likely by ourselves. The places where we feel most broken often don't need to be fixed. What they need is to be heard.

Finding Your Tribe

Finally, we arrive at perhaps the most important element of wiser self-protection: finding the people who value your deepest nature, and toward whom you feel the same. Let me share a story to introduce this idea.

In a certain East African tribe, conception is counted from the day when a mother first has the thought of her child. When this happens, she goes to sit under a tree to listen for the spirit song of her unborn child. When the mother hears and learns the child's song, she goes back and teaches it to her husband, and they teach it to the midwife, and then to the whole village. When the child is born, she enters the world hearing that song. At birthdays, festivals, and other life milestones, the village sings this song to the child. And for the rest of the child's life, in times of deep crisis or transition, members of the village will sing this song to her, knowing that in hearing her own song, she will find a path through her suffering.[2]

I think this story captures a beautiful vision of how self-love is born and nurtured through relationships. We all need to be reminded that we have a song and that it is good and worthy of hearing. We don't learn that lesson through willpower or through forced "positive thinking." We learn it through intimacy. And, as the story of the spirit song illustrates, our song is born and reborn with the support of others.

Everyone's heard the self-help platitude "You must love yourself before you can love anyone else." This may sound wise, but it misses a great truth: if we want to experience true intimacy, we need to be *taught* to love aspects of ourselves—again and again—by the people around us. As much as most of us want to control our own destiny, the humbling truth is that sometimes the only way to learn self-love is by *being* loved—precisely in the parts of ourselves where we feel most unsure and tender. When we are loved in such a way, we feel freedom and relief and permission to love in a deeper way. No amount of positive self-talk can replicate this experience.

It is a gift of intimacy, not of willpower. When we surround our-selves with people who honor our gifts and whose gifts we also honor, our lives blossom.

Yet if our vulnerability is met with derision or disinterest, some-thing tender shrivels and retracts within us, and we may think twice about ever sharing that part of ourselves again. Every time we face the choice to share our deeper self, we stand at a precipice. Often, it's just too scary to take the step forward.

Imagine taking a pet you love and putting it in a yard with an invisible electric fence. When it moves outside its allowed space, it gets stunned by a mild but unexpected shock. It will only take a few jolts before your pet gets the message: if it goes too far, punishment will be instantaneous. In a short period of time, your pet will act as if the borders don't even exist; it will simply avoid them. If pushed closer to the danger zone, your pet will exhibit increasing signs of anxiety. The world outside the fence just isn't worth the pain.

Now imagine turning off the charge from the invisible fence, and then placing a bowl of food outside its perimeter. Your pet might be hungry, but it will still be afraid to cross into the newly freed space. When it finally does cross the line to get to the tempt-ing bowl of food, it does so trembling, anticipating the discomfort of new shocks. It is the same with us. Even though we yearn for the freedom of experiencing our true selves, a deep reflexive instinct still tries to protect us from being hurt again.

This shame around our most vulnerable attributes is almost uni-versal. And even our strongest willpower will barely budge it. So how can we free ourselves from the thrall of learned shame and fear around our gifts? The best—and sometimes the *only*—way out is through relationships that instruct us in the worth of our most vulnerable self.

Of all the people you know, who sees and relishes your true self? Who is not afraid of your passion or envious of your gifts? Who has the generosity of spirit to encourage you toward greater self-expression? These people are your gold. Practice leaning on them more, and giving more back to them.

You may think that a community of loved ones can come later; that what you really need is a partner. If you think this way, chances are good that you are sabotaging your search for love. If you seek romantic love but are not building love into your relationships with friends and family, chances are good that you won't find what you're looking for. In a talk I attended by the renowned spiritual teacher Marianne Williamson, I remember her saying, "The more I grow, the more my friends become like lovers and my lovers become like friends."

Our characters are like wax. Left alone in the cold commerce of day-to-day life, we harden into whatever shape our environment creates for us. Wax must be warmed to be reshaped. We are warmed when we are in the Gift Zone. When we are in the presence of people with whom we feel safe, we are also warmed. We begin to soften. We find ourselves becoming malleable and trusting as we open these tender parts of ourselves again. At that time we need the kind and supportive hands of others to help us reshape ourselves. We can't do it alone.

MICRO-MEDITATION

Your Intimacy Heroes | Two minutes

Who in your life has appreciated your Core Gifts? Who has seen these deep qualities in you and shown you that they were good and valuable? This person may never have used the word gift, *but the way he or she treated you made you feel the value of these parts of you. My grandmother played that role for me. She never used the word* gift, *but through her kind and caring actions she taught me about a quality of goodness that she and I shared.*

Who comes to mind for you? What was the quality this person saw and appreciated in you? Which of your Core Gifts were seen and validated by this person? How did this change the course of your life? Silently or aloud, find the

*words to thank this person for what he or she gave you. Feel
the ripples this meditation brings up for you.*

YOUR GIFT CIRCLE

This brings us to one of the most important and life-affirming processes in Deeper Dating: the Gift Circle. Your Gift Circle will be a
curated group of people who know you well and who will give you
invaluable insights about your Core Gifts. You may be astounded
by how many new and important things you will learn about yourself from your Gift Circle. And you'll probably be amazed by the
amount of pleasure and sense of empowerment this process gives
you. Here are some quotes from people who created their own Gift
Circles:

- "I am going through my days with a deep sense of happiness. I
  don't think I ever understood my Core Gifts in the way I do now."

- "I never realized how loved and respected I am, and it's changed
  the way I feel about myself."

- "I laughed, I cried, I felt *seen* like never before. Thank you for this."

How to Create Your Gift Circle

For your Gift Circle try to think of four to six people who are safest
for you, who know you most deeply, and whose insights you value.
Invite these people to be a part of your Gift Circle. You can write to
them or talk to them in person or over the phone. If you are writing
to your Gift Circle, see "Sample Letter to Gift Circle Helpers," on
pages 241–42, to help get you started. You can also use this letter as
an aid in deciding what to say when you speak to people.

There are many ways to do a Gift Circle, so find a way that
works best for you. Ideally, you can all get together in person. But
you can also do a Gift Circle through a conference call, in separate

meetings or calls, through one-on-one e-mails, or via group e-mails so that the members of your circle can see what other people wrote and build upon that. (The downside of e-mails is that the impact of the experience might be a bit diminished. The upside is that it's easier to do, and you'll always have what people have written to you.) This process might take a few weeks to complete, given how full many people's schedules are.

Explain to the members of your Gift Circle that you are working to deepen and expand the intimacy in your life. Ask each person to describe the qualities they most respect and appreciate about you. Suggest that they try to describe the essence of your spirit, the things they most treasure about you. The main rule in a Gift Circle is that *only* positive feedback is allowed. Please be sure that everyone in your group understands and agrees to this ground rule. Sure, there are things you need to change, but this exercise is for the purpose of helping you to understand and appreciate your gifts in a deeper way.

In my experience, most people undervalue and underappreciate their gifts. Often, it takes a loved one's descriptions of our gifts to awaken us to them. In some cases, our gifts are so obvious to us, so basic, that we don't even see them as gifts. "Isn't everyone that way?" we ask. In our Gift Circle, we see that the qualities we've often taken for granted have actually affected other people's lives in powerful ways. Often, our Core Gifts are entangled with our perceived imperfections—the things we get most mad at ourselves for or feel most insecure about. If that is the case we need an outside person to remind us of the deep strands of beauty that shine in our imperfect humanity.

Furthermore, when we hear someone else name our Core Gifts, we begin to understand the ways life has hurt us most deeply around our gifts, and we gain a new appreciation of how these gifts have shaped our lives.

Take these appreciations to heart. They are real, and you have earned them. My guess is that your commitment to live those gifts has caused you pain, and has entailed hard work. You have a right to feel gratified when they are acknowledged. The more you acknowledge the precious worth of your gifts, the more you will express them. And the more you express them, the more love you will find.

You may find that you shut down when you receive your positive feedback, especially if it's being offered to you verbally instead of through e-mail. The positive feedback may be too hard to take, or to believe. Don't worry—this is normal. Many of the ideas will still get through.

When each member is finished, give the same thing back to your Gift Circle members, if they want it. Describe the gifts that you see in them. This will help you integrate the entire experience.

The experience of having your gifts reflected to you can feel like a map emerging from out of the haze, a map of who you are and of the possibilities of who you can become. When you have a positive sense of who you are, you can more easily find the energy to cut through the obstacles, fears, and fogs that separate you from love.

If you don't feel ready to undertake a full Gift Circle, try doing it with just one person. If that still feels too difficult, you can also try this modification: Write a letter to yourself that you imagine might be written by a loved one or a group of loved ones. Even though it's from you, it may well have the ring of truth and thus be helpful for you.

Creating your own Gift Circle will seem daunting and awkward. Just take that for granted and try to jump in. The joy and meaning you will get from this life-changing experience will be worth every drop of discomfort you may feel in setting it up.

Deeper Dating Workbook

PERSONAL EXERCISES

Your Gift Circle

Your main exercise for this lesson will be to build and create your Gift Circle. Think of how you would like to plan it, whom you wish to include in it, and how you want to arrange the logistics for it to happen.

DEEPER DATING EXERCISE
The Gift You Feel Timid about Showing

In this chapter, I asked you to identify a gift that you often suppress. These suppressed gifts are often particularly important in our search for love. This week your task is to try to gently reveal that part of yourself on any dates you have, and to use the skills of discrimination to see with whom that gift feels safe. When you find someone who appreciates your gifts, whether or not she or he becomes "the one," you'll experience a sense of freedom and comfort. If you are not dating anyone at this moment, practice this exercise with anyone you sense will respond positively. Write down your reflections on how it felt to reveal this part of yourself and what outcomes you experienced.

LEARNING PARTNER EXERCISE
Create Your Gift Circle

Work with your learning partner to make a list of people to invite into your Gift Circle. Support each other in reaching out to these people and initiating your Gift Circles. As you both get your Gift Circle responses, share them with each other. Try to articulate the most important Core Gift that was revealed to each of you in this process.

Recognize Which Attractions Lead to Love and Which Lead to Pain

In the three preceding chapters you began the process of discovering and naming your Core Gifts. Now we will move into the second stage of your journey. In this stage you'll bring your Core Gifts into your dating life in ways that may create a sea change in your search for love. You'll learn new ways to understand your romantic and sexual attractions, and I'll explain what I have found to be the most important principle for finding inspiring, lasting love.

With that knowledge you'll be able to chart a path to a much happier future in love. Finally, you'll learn two exquisitely simple yet profound techniques for tapping into the deepest roots of your being to help guide your search for love.

The Old Map to Love

The more intense your immediate attractions, the more powerful your future love and passion will be. In most cases, it's immediately obvious who attracts you. Barring any red flags, that's the person to go for. Why spend your future with someone who doesn't turn you on?

The New Map to Love

Often, our wildest attractions are actually warning signs that forecast unavailability and emotional risk. In contrast, many healthy, loving, and passionate lasting relationships begin in a gentler way and get more intense over time. We haven't been taught that we can *grow* our sexual and romantic passion. "We can make people practically fall in love," says the psychologist Arthur Aron. In a well-known experiment, he and four colleagues put strangers into pairs and had them answer questions that required them to share increasingly vulnerable aspects of themselves. In addition, both members of the pair were asked to reveal what they liked most about each other. These actions created a powerful increase in levels of attraction between partners.[1]

Other studies prove that activities such as eye gazing, gentle touch, laughter, breathing in synchronicity, engaging in exciting and novel activities, and making a commitment to the relationship all tend to increase romantic and sexual desire.[2] We can consciously cultivate deeper states of sexual and romantic turn-on. Sadly, almost none of us has been taught how to do this.

4

Attractions of Inspiration and Attractions of Deprivation

The Most Important Distinction of All

> Be with those who help your being.
> —RUMI

Our attractions are forged in the deep space of our being. They are born of countless, often unknowable forces, including psychological, evolutionary, and biological influences. How we respond to them will shape much of our future—the quality of our days, the degree of happiness and intimacy in our lives, and perhaps even the mark we leave upon the world.

We all know how much our erotic and romantic attractions drive our relationships. Yet we're sent out into the world of dating without ever being taught how to work with their tremendous power. Much of what we learn is superficial, naive, or downright untrue. With a fuller understanding of our attractions we can save ourselves vast amounts of time and suffering in our search for real and lasting love.

UNDERSTANDING ATTRACTION

Imagine being guided into a room with a beautiful, sophisticated lighting console that allows you to play with myriad shapes of light and an almost endless variety of colors, each with numerous intensities and tones. That's the richness of possibility available to us with our sexual, sensual, spiritual, and emotional attractions.

Now imagine that your guide moves you past this splendid console, to a simple, dusty on-off switch. Two choices: on or off. That's all you get.

This is the way we have been taught to understand our attractions. You're either attracted to someone right now, or you won't ever be. There's no recognition of how the quality of our connection with someone affects our attraction to them, or of the factors that make passion grow or dissipate. Limited as we are by our culture's poverty of insight about attractions, many of us simply follow our most intense attractions and hope we'll be lucky enough to fall for someone loyal, honest, kind, and accomplished—who loves us back. In most cases, this approach offers the same odds of success as a Las Vegas slot machine. A slot machine, however, can only rob us of money. An unwise choice in love robs us of joy, well-being, and a happy future for ourselves, our partner, and our children. If we want to create a future of lasting love, we must develop a more sophisticated understanding of how our attractions work, and how we can work with them.

For example, Ann was attracted to guys who were somewhat arrogant, but she didn't appreciate being treated disrespectfully by anyone—least of all by her boyfriend! That was the main reason all her relationships ended. Still, cocky guys turned her on in a visceral way, and nice guys just didn't. She really wanted a husband and family, but she knew she couldn't settle for a marriage with someone she wasn't attracted to. It was a real problem: the people she was attracted to weren't marriage material, and the ones who were marriage material didn't excite her.

If you relate to Ann's predicament, you certainly are not alone. This quandary plagues the lives of countless single people.

Three Insights about Attractions

There is an art to working with our attractions that most of us have never been taught. The following three insights offer a sense of the possibilities available to us as we approach our attractions in a wiser way.

First, our attractions—both healthy and unhealthy—reveal our Core Gifts and the quality of our relationship to those gifts. For example, the less we value a particular Core Gift, the more we will be attracted to people who also devalue that gift. Conversely, the more we value a particular gift, the more we will be attracted to people who also value that gift; people who can help that gift come alive and feel safe in the world. The types of people we are repeatedly attracted to reveal essential information about who we are. *Our attractions can educate us.*

Second, we can actually change and shape our sexual and romantic attractions. We can never change them by force, but we can form a wiser alliance with them. In fact, as you learn to honor your Core Gifts you will find something amazing begin to happen: your attractions will actually start to change. You will gradually become more attracted to people who know how to cherish your deep innate qualities and you'll lose your taste for people who try to diminish them. *We can educate our attractions.*

Third, there is an invaluable guiding principle that can change your entire search for love: learn the difference between your "attractions of inspiration" and your "attractions of deprivation." Then, *only* follow your attractions of inspiration. This is the wisest path to love. But wise doesn't mean easy. Attractions of deprivation can be wildly compelling, posing as true love as they woo us off the edge of a cliff. And attractions of inspiration hold challenges that few of us are trained to meet. Knowing how to distinguish between these two attractions enables us to steer our search for love in a much wiser way. *We can use our attractions to guide us toward lasting love.*

Attractions of Deprivation

Have you ever been crazy about someone who wasn't really emotionally available? Have you ever invested far too much time trying to teach someone to treat you right? Have you ever continually tried to prove your worth to someone who never really thought you were that wonderful? Or felt desperate for the affection of someone who sometimes treated you wonderfully, and other times badly? If you haven't, come introduce yourself; I don't think we've met yet. These attractions can be the most desperately compelling of all.

All of us are attracted to a certain type that can knock us off balance: a physical type, an emotional type, and a personality type. These "iconic" attractions can make us weak in the knees, and they trigger our insecurities as well as our longing. Frequently they end in pain, for reasons we'll explore in greater detail in this chapter and later ones.

Attractions of deprivation draw us in—and then *down*, just like an undertow. If we don't get out in time, we're almost sure to get hurt. We keep feeling we have to *do* something to win our partner's love, approval, or care. We spend way too much time worrying about what we've done wrong, or what we can do differently to make things right. These relationships can trigger a sense of need and longing that robs us of our balance. With some attractions of deprivation, we see the red flags early on but can't stop ourselves. With others, the deprivational aspects of the relationship don't reveal themselves right away.

Meryl, a thirty-five-year-old guidance counselor in the public school system, felt happier than she had ever been. She was deeply in love with her fiancé, Jeff, a handsome, highly successful real estate developer who volunteered as a mentor for underprivileged youth. He was brilliant, generous, and sure of himself. From all appearances he was as devoted to her as she was to him, and they spent many hours sharing dreams of a future together. The sex was magical; at times it felt transcendent.

Jeff had come into Meryl's life at a time when she was very vulnerable. She had just been through a series of family tragedies, including the death of her brother. Jeff's assured presence and his promises of a loving, secure future fed her deepest needs. She loved him with an intensity that sometimes scared her. And she believed beyond a doubt that he loved her just as much.

Over time, however, emerging patterns in the relationship began to bother her. She didn't want to believe that their future was in jeopardy, but she knew that these problems were serious. For one, the balance of power was off. Jeff always needed to be the authority. He seldom went to her place; his was, after all, much more beautiful. Her friends noticed—and told her—that Jeff's generosity and brilliance were often used to impress others. He loved to talk about himself and he would subtly criticize her appearance, mannerisms, home decor, and friends. Jeff was the greatest love of her life, yet she found herself in pain all too often.

Meryl had an extraordinary capacity to give to those around her. Her gifts were quiet ones; she had no interest in making a fuss about herself. Jeff had to be in the center of things, and it mattered a great deal to him that he was perceived as brilliant, even heroic. She and Jeff would laugh about what they called the "creative tension" between their personalities. Even so, Meryl began to feel "less than" in the relationship. She often had to defend herself against his subtle criticisms, and she kept feeling that she had to prove her loyalty to him.

Frustrated, she persuaded Jeff to go into couples counseling. Though he agreed to attend, he wasn't willing to do the hard work of healing. It was too threatening to his sense of self. In a stunning moment of anger, he abruptly ended the therapy with no warning and no closure, blaming Meryl's oversensitivity for their problems.

Meryl was devastated. It felt as if her dreams were collapsing around her. In the end, she left him. The decision to leave was anguishing, because Jeff's goodness was real, and many aspects of their relationship were passionate and joyful. Yet ultimately it had become a relationship of pain and wounding. When she began to heal from the pain of her loss, she could see the signs she hadn't wanted to face. In essential ways, this was an attraction of deprivation.

Trying to get love from people who don't treasure our gifts is usually an exercise in self-punishment. In addition to the pain of the relationship, there is a secondary cost: they imprint upon us that our gifts, those most sacred and essential parts of ourselves, are somehow flawed and shameful.

If these attractions are so painful, why isn't it easier to break free of them? One reason is that attractions of deprivation are what behavioral theorists call "intermittent reward systems." In these systems you get rewarded only sporadically and you can't control when the reward will come. Intermittent reward systems are the most compelling form of reinforcement and the hardest to break free of. Gambling is a perfect example of an intermittent reward system.

Following are six major signs of an attraction of deprivation. As you read and think about them in connection with others, I encourage you to also consider whether you engage in any of these intimacy-sabotaging behaviors.

Lying and cheating. If you can't trust your partner's integrity, you do not have a solid foundation for a healthy and happy future together. Period.

Selfish behavior. Generosity is the medium in which love grows. All of us are selfish in one way or another. Yet if you don't feel an essential quality of generosity of spirit from your partner, this is a sign of an attraction of deprivation.

Unavailability. We can't expect our partner to precisely match our level of availability. However, if a partner remains unwilling to commit over time, is still with someone else, or continually switches from being interested to being unavailable, beware. These are major signs of an attraction of deprivation.

Addictive behavior. If the person you're dating has an active addiction, this is a matter of serious concern. If your partner is not willing to get help, I encourage you to move on—or at least not to move to the next level of commitment—unless your partner gets serious, ongoing help and remains clean and sober for a good period of time.

Hurtful behavior. If the person you are dating is emotionally hurtful, if he or she subtly or blatantly degrades, criticizes, or minimizes your ideas, your behaviors, your friends, your career, or your physical attributes, this is a relationship to stay away from. Often, this kind of behavior alternates with affection, compliments, and generosity, so it becomes even more "crazy-making." If this person is physically abusive, I cannot urge you strongly enough to get help—and get out. Right away.

Untreated or unresolved emotional or psychological disorders. If the person you're dating has bipolar tendencies, serious depression, or any of a wide range of significant psychological problems, it's not the end of the world—unless he or she refuses to get help appropriate to the severity of his or her condition. If the condition is serious and she or he refuses adequate help, assume that your future as a couple will be an unhappy one.

Blaming and manipulative behavior. If the person you're dating is frequently blaming, manipulative, and punishing, assume that these traits will only grow stronger in time, unless he or she is making a real effort to change.

After decades of witnessing many breakups, I'd like to offer a somber warning: if you are embarking upon a relationship with a person who has an untreated and significant psychological disorder or an active addiction, and is not willing to get serious and adequate help, I encourage you to assume that this relationship will fail, and probably in a very painful way.

To some degree, we all exhibit some of the attributes just listed, and no matter how good our partners are, we will still be hurt and let down by them at times. All relationships go through a process that the psychiatrist Daniel J. Siegel calls "rupture and repair."[1] The connection gets broken, and both parties struggle to find the tools to fix things between them. Rupture occurs at the gap between differing perspectives and conflicting needs. When we face each other, my right will always be your left. Rupture comes naturally in relationships, and usually it hurts. In a healthy relationship, repair is possible when both parties care enough to do the work. Attractions of deprivation are dysfunctional beyond the normal ruptures that occur in all relationships.

Attractions of Deprivation Are a Flight from Intimacy

Attractions of deprivation are also one of the trickiest ways to flee real intimacy. In these relationships our fear of intimacy is hiding in plain sight. We're desperately seeking a solid love—from someone who we know, deep down, won't give it to us. With an attraction of deprivation, in some odd way we are *safe*. I've found that the people most drawn to attractions of deprivation experience discomfort, fear, unworthiness, or anger when they are confronted with a kind, stable, and available partner. *The more we are drawn to attractions of deprivation, the less we will feel comfortable with available and caring people.* Many of us need to develop our *taste* for healthy, stable relationships.

Attractions of deprivation are frequently birthed by our fear of our own power and, oftentimes, our fear of love. At bottom they are distractions from the scariest things of all: the challenge of our gifts in our lives, and the challenges inherent in a healthy relationship. As long as we're focusing on getting someone else to love us right, we won't have the time—or the sense of self—to live our deepest sense of mission. A bad relationship gives us a hall pass from facing the challenge of our authentic struggles, and it comes complete with the sympathy of loved ones!

Meryl fled the challenges of her own life for Jeff's illusory protection, and she ultimately had to come back to the truth of her own life, one that felt terribly empty—of her brother, and now of Jeff. But it was *her* life, and after leaving Jeff, she remembered how good it felt to claim it. She knew that she would never again get involved with someone who needed to bolster his ego by diminishing her sense of self-worth. Her gifts may have been less obvious and flashy than Jeff's accomplishments, but they were real gifts, and she had learned how important it was to be with a man who valued them.

Like Meryl, the more we dishonor our gifts, the more we will be attracted to people who agree that our gifts *deserve* to be dishonored. The more extreme your shame or ambivalence about a Core Gift, the more you'll be attracted to partners who disdain or neglect that gift. Unconsciously we act out a denigration of every important part of our self that we haven't learned to accept. This is a very important concept. It means that you can assess how much you value your Core Gifts by the partners you choose.

Relationships of deprivation actually reinforce that our gifts, the most precious and valuable parts of ourselves, are inherently unworthy. In the next chapter we will explore the roots of these attractions in greater detail.

Breaking the Cycle of Deprivational Attractions

For Meryl, letting go of her painful relationship was immensely difficult. Most of us have a very hard time leaving a bad relationship, because we feel we'll be left with nothing. Separation is usually a much slower and more agonizing process than we might imagine.

Part of us holds on to attractions of deprivation because they seem so close to the real love we're looking for. But we must gently and repeatedly be brought back to true relationships of inspiration until those begin to feel both comfortable and desirable. If you find yourself trapped in an attraction of deprivation, you should rally all the inner and outer support you can get. Go for couples counseling if you feel there's hope for the relationship and you really want to pursue it. Engage the help and support of friends. Look into twelve-step meetings, coaching, or psychotherapy. If the relationship doesn't change, then you may need to think about leaving. Often we can't take that step on our own. If you want to end a relationship, find all the help and support you can get, before, during, and after the breakup.

Breakups from attractions of deprivation can often leave us feeling shame for having fallen for someone who, in hindsight, turned out to be wrong for us. Take the words of the psychotherapist and Deeper Dating instructor Kathryn Janus to heart: "After a breakup, clients may say something like, 'I feel like such an idiot. I can't believe I loved someone like that! What was I thinking?' My response is always: 'What did you do that was so horrible? You loved someone. That's a good thing. You'll use this relationship as a learning opportunity that will inform whom you choose in the future. You may choose differently next time. But never shame yourself for loving someone. Never.'"[2]

Attractions of Inspiration

Now we come to the simplest path toward happiness in love. The great secret to finding lasting love lies in choosing and cultivating only attractions of inspiration. Only. It's so simple, yet it takes decades for most of us to arrive at this truth, if we ever do at all. Attractions of deprivation rarely become relationships of inspiration, even with love, commitment, and lots of work. We don't need the roller coaster of negative attractions in order to grow! We can grow through inspiration instead.

Attractions of inspiration have a warmth and an easiness. In these relationships, our challenge is to accept and return our partner's caring, not to *win* that caring. Our partners might challenge us to be better, but at bottom, they love us for who we are. Attractions of inspiration are fueled by the real sense of well-being that the relationship creates in us, not by the unrelenting itch for something that's denied us. These attractions often unfold slowly. They get richer as time goes on. They may take lots of work—but such relationships *allow* the work of intimacy. They make us feel love, not desperation. These are the only relationships to build a life around, the only ones that deserve the gift of our most intimate self. And I promise you, they really are out there.

We can measure the quality of our lives by the relationships of mutual inspiration we've cultivated. These are the relationships that allow us to trust life. They are the very foundation of joy. Without such inspiration, any love will wither. And without these relationships, we too will wither, reverting to smaller, more defensive and wounded versions of ourselves. Humans are a lot like rubber bands: we shrink to a small, comfortable size unless we're held to greater expansion by forces outside ourselves. Relationships of inspiration expand us to a size we could never achieve alone.

These relationships are not only the path to love; they are the path to our own greatness. Through them we can find a way past the fears and wounds that dwarf us. Popular psychology tells us that we can only love others if we love ourselves first. But the real truth is often the other way around: until we feel seen and loved in the places we're most vulnerable (usually the places of our deepest gifts), few of us will ever be able to fully love ourselves. That's the great boon of relationships of inspiration. We experience our loved one seeing into our very core—and valuing what he sees. In the wake of this experience comes a sense of bravery, an innate desire to share our gifts—not out of obligation but from a sense of joyful overflow. And that makes us into just the kind of person we are looking for—one who inspires others simply by who she is.

Here are some markers for identifying your attractions of inspiration:

- Are you inspired by your partner's (mostly) consistent caring and acceptance?

- Are you inspired by your partner's goodness, decency, and integrity?

- Is your love fueled by respect for the kind of person your partner is?

- Are you and your partner willing to do the hard work of healing the relationship's areas of weakness?

- Do you like who you are in the presence of your partner? Does he or she make you a better you?

- Is your partner essentially free of the qualities of attractions of deprivation listed on pages 86–87?

If you can answer yes to these questions, celebrate. You have found an attraction of inspiration, and you should treasure it. It's the type that can sustain a future of love. Of course, no attraction is purely one of inspiration. Nothing is black and white. However, we want to choose relationships where the degree of inspiration is high and the degree of deprivation in the most important areas is relatively low.

Relationships of inspiration are not just for the lucky. We all can find these relationships by dating in wiser ways. The first step on this path is to develop an "eye for inspiration"; in other words, *to look for inspiration at least as much as we look for sexual attraction*. This next micro-meditation will help you recognize and embrace your attractions of inspiration, including nonromantic ones. Try it for a day—or better yet, try it every day—and enjoy the lessons it imparts.

MICRO-MEDITATION

Savoring Inspiration | One minute

You can do this micro-meditation anytime you're moved by someone's kindness, exuberance, warmth, creativity, or any other positive attribute. Whenever that happens, don't just notice it and move on. Take an extra moment to savor the good feeling you get inside. Let it linger, casting its ripples inside you. For example, a store attendant showing extra kindness and patience to an elderly shopper, a parent laughing together with his child, or a stranger smiling at you in the street. In the warmth that you feel after these tiny moments of humanity, you'll catch a glimpse of your own gifts. At those times, feel the warming pleasure that has just been sparked inside you. Enjoy this miniature meditation every time you experience moments of inspiration, and then move on with your day, a bit richer each time. The more you do this exercise, the happier you'll find yourself, and the better you'll become at recognizing signs of inspiration.

Cultivating Attractions of Inspiration

What happens when we meet someone who inspires us, and we feel some spark of attraction but not enough to fall in love? It's important to understand this point: attractions of inspiration present themselves differently than attractions of deprivation. Don't expect to feel the same wild-fire sense of attraction with someone kind and available that you would with an intense attraction of deprivation. Sometimes we feel an immediate, weak-kneed desire for an attraction of inspiration—and that's great! However, don't discount an attraction as less worthy just because it begins with more warmth than fire. You can experience "like at first sight" and have it grow into love. Many—perhaps most—people who are in relationships did not experience love at first sight with each other; the feelings grew as they got to know each other.[3] I'm not advising you to "settle" for an attraction that isn't strong simply because the person is good for you. I'm simply coaching you to recognize the difference between fool's gold and real gold, and then to decide for yourself. The most wonderful love of all is when our partner's decency, integrity, and commitment make our heart feel full, and when our sex life ignites *because* of that. Then we know we have found a good and true love. This is not about settling. In fact, it's about finding what you've been dreaming of.

Is there a sensual or sexual spark with this person? Is there a growing sense of warmth and pleasure? Is your heart touched? If so, you may very possibly have found someone wonderful. Don't make the mistake of fleeing because you're judging this quieter attraction against the wild thrill of getting an unavailable or unhealthy person to love you for a little while. Such intensity makes us feel shaky and unbalanced. Ultimately, we find we have wasted time, lost our center, and denigrated our gifts in order to keep the relationship going.

In reality, sexual attraction is much more mutable than we've been taught. Sure, we all have types that turn us on immediately and intensely. But attractions can grow. I'm not saying you'll become attracted to someone who isn't physically appealing to you. But if someone holds a spark of attraction for you, and has other qualities you love, your attraction can blossom. When you meet someone for the first time, don't make a snap decision on the basis of an instant physical attraction. If you're not sure, just keep dating. In time, something lovely may happen: your attraction may grow in surprising ways. And if not, you'll know that it's time to stop dating that person.

Mark and his wife have one of the strongest relationships I know. The bedrock of their bond lies in a rock-solid commitment to openness, honesty, and their couplehood, even when that's really hard to do. Here's their story:

Mark had a tough upbringing. His mother died when he was young and his dad was very passive. Mark had no real mentors, no guides to help him get through the trauma of the loss of his mother. His life felt like a constant struggle until he found his calling as a physical therapist. That's when he met Sarah.

Mark had only been practicing for about six months when he got his first referral to work with someone at home. The first session was terrible. In his words, "I knocked on the door and there was this woman with a little girl next to her. She actually ordered me around, telling me how to work on her. There was no physical attraction for either of us. She was quite difficult." Mark never thought the arrangement would last.

Well, it did last. They've been together twenty-two years and counting.

"That door I knocked on? That was the door of the house I'm standing in right now, twenty-two years later. And that little girl is now my stepdaughter, and I have a stepson as well."

As they worked, Sarah and Mark grew very close, but it was

strictly platonic. They became each other's best friend. One day, something shifted without their even realizing it. They looked at each other in a strange way, and that was it. Lust was in full bloom — and it was amazing for both of them. After that, Sarah started to get serious about Mark, but Mark was sure she wasn't a good match for him. He was used to dating stunning model types, and Sarah, though attractive, was not a model type. He didn't want to settle. Attraction was too important. Great friends, yes. Great sex, yes. But marriage? No way!

Mark says, "Now I can admit that I was a shallow person. I wasn't in touch with my intimate feelings. I wasn't in touch with love. And now all of a sudden I was starting to feel deeply for this person. I was completely confused. One part of me felt, 'Wow, she's amazing, she makes me happy. I have this incredible friendship and fantastic sex with her. She's so smart. I feel so good around her, I feel so empowered and so great.' And the other part knew I wasn't physically attracted to her enough. That was huge for me."

Mark was in such turmoil that he knew he had to go back to therapy to work on this issue. He had to face that the issue was rooted in his need to build his self-esteem by having someone attractive on his arm. There was so much rich love, intimacy, and sexual adventurousness with Sarah. Mark knew that if he could work through this and break through his barrier, it would make him a better person and that he would have a happier life. That was the guy he wanted to be. But Mark wasn't that guy yet.

"The pain was so powerful, I can't explain it," Mark said. "I was killing myself thinking, 'How can I let this relationship die?' It was like a roller coaster every day. Because if I didn't marry her, I didn't know what would happen to me. She completed me. She made me a better person. And I knew we would both flourish further if we could be together. But that one hang-up about looks was so powerful that I couldn't shake it."

Finally, Mark just broke it off. He told Sarah, "I just can't do it." Sarah agreed that it wasn't working and that it was time to stop trying. They spent three months apart. After about a month or two, they didn't even e-mail. They were over. Mark barely even thought about her.

Sarah went through her own tumultuous journey as she wrestled with her relationship to Mark. She had previously been in a very painful marriage, and had finally ended it. In retrospect, she sees that though she was brave enough to end the marriage, she was still looking for a Prince Charming to save her. Mark may have wanted a swimsuit model, but Sarah wanted a successful guy with a lot of money. For two years she and Mark had been on again, off again. At a certain point they stopped telling their friends when they were breaking up or getting back together because they felt they had lost all legitimacy as a couple. When Sarah agreed with Mark that they should end it for good, she warned him not to come back unless he was 100 percent ready to get married. And when she did that, a calm came over her that she hadn't felt in years.

Sarah says, "When I broke up with Mark, that's when I finally felt like I was steering my own ship. I really was great with the kids. I became a much better mother, I just became much more relaxed. And surprisingly enough—I guess it's not that surprising—I became very popular. I started dating like crazy."

One of the people Sarah dated was getting very serious about her. He even wanted to marry her. Sarah wasn't ready, but she was happy with how things were going—with him, and in her life as a whole. Mark was content too—until his whole world changed.

To this day Mark is still shaken as he remembers what happened next. He was back in his apartment with an old girlfriend of his. She was stunning, and the sex was great, but there was nothing of substance there. It was about one o'clock in the morning, and Mark was fast asleep. All of a sudden he woke up, startled. It was as if someone started shaking him, saying, "What are you doing, Mark? What are you doing?" He jerked awake, in a cold sweat. He remembers his sense of panic as he thought, "Oh, my God, what have I done? I've lost Sarah." He asked himself over and over again, "What am I going to do?"

This is what Mark did: First thing in the morning, he grabbed his best friend to shop for a ring. Then he rushed to Sarah's house to propose to her. Sarah turned him down—for about thirty minutes. She was still angry, but she knew she loved him, and she knew he loved her kids. The marriage was for all four of them, and she knew it was what they all wanted.

Remembering his experience that night, Mark says, "I believe it was my mother who shook me awake. She died when I was really young. I could feel that this person who 'shook me' cared deeply about me and my life. It was as if she were saying, 'Listen, wake up. You'd better get over there fast or your life is not going to be what it could be.' And I felt my mother's presence."

Mark had one more thing he wanted to tell me: "Once I made that decision, the roller coaster ended for me. I didn't feel that anguish anymore. I look at Sarah today and she's twenty years older than when I was having concerns about her appearance. She's older, she's not as toned; that's just what happens with age. I'm not blind to reality. Yet it doesn't bother me. I love her more than ever. I love her completely.

"But it wasn't an intellectual choice. That's the beauty of it. I believe that what happened with me is that I *changed*. I was willing to really look deep into myself and grow. My choice made me so much of a better person. I almost spent my whole life trying to pick the person who fit my exact physical type, and in the end, it wouldn't have meant anything. I've grown so much over the last twenty years, and I continue to grow, and it's because I have the person of my dreams who is helping me grow. That's the most important thing of all."

CHOOSING HAPPINESS:
INSPIRATION VS. DEPRIVATION

Attractions of inspiration rarely spin us into a state of obsession. As with Mark and Sarah, their power is based upon connection, not unavailability. Attractions of deprivation often feel euphorically exciting, they make us feel alive. The longing for what we don't have and the desperate need to earn our worth and value can be compelling beyond imagination. Many of us believe that attractions of deprivation are real love, because they draw us in so powerfully. When these attractions invariably let us down, we believe it's because of a lack in us, not because of a fatal flaw embedded in the attractions themselves.

Sandy, a patient who had been in a series of deprivational relationships, had essentially sworn off romance. The men she fell for were always still in love with their ex-wives, unsure of their sexuality, or otherwise unavailable. Therefore, she decided that she would devote her attention to her successful restaurant and give up on men for the time being. She preferred being lonely to being in pain—and she knew that the men she chose ultimately brought her pain. One day in therapy, she had an important epiphany. She realized that while her most intense attractions were toward unavailable men, she could also be attracted to positive qualities. She was drawn to guys who couldn't commit, yes; but she was *also* drawn to qualities of kindness, decency—and availability. She remembered one boyfriend whose love of food inspired her to become a chef, and how consistently supportive and caring he was of her—and she *still* fell in love with him! That meant she was capable of falling in love for the *right* reasons. The problem was that she kept looking for turn-on first, and inspiration later.

Simply put, her order was off. Turn-on is simple; it takes care of itself. Noticing inspiration requires time and a conscious decision to look for it. Of course, she had to be physically attracted to someone, but she was sure that there were men out there who both attracted and inspired her.

Sandy's realization was profound. She realized that she had two totally different systems of wiring—and that she could choose which to follow. She could follow her compelling, scratch-the-itch attractions of deprivation, or she could follow attractions that fed the best parts of her. And from that point on, she began to look for people who inspired her with their goodness. Only. That's when her dating life really began to change.

Most of us are wired to want the hard-to-get. When someone doesn't completely desire us, we unconsciously grant him or her a special mystique. People who devalue us make us want to convince them of our worth. These are our circuitries of deprivation.

But—and here's the all-important part—we also have the circuitry to become attracted to people who inspire us, value us, and are available. Just because we have a hair-trigger attraction to negative relationships doesn't mean that we can't be deeply attracted to inspiring ones. We've just never been taught that we can choose the healthier love, and then consciously cultivate its passion and sexual heat.

We all have two circuitries: attraction to deprivation and attraction to inspiration. Both can lead to deep attachment. It's just that the former is likely to lead to emotional hell, and the latter can lead to a future of love and overall happiness. This is true in friendships and it's true in the search for a partner. And it's a truth that isn't taught. Making the decision to invest only in attractions of inspiration affects whom we notice and actually begins to change our attractions—as you'll see.

THE 90 PERCENT RULE

I often tell clients about the 90 percent rule: At least 90 percent of the people you meet—including those with whom there is some mutual chemistry—won't be a match. Your deepest gifts just won't feel safe or right with them. The goal is not to become tougher and more thick-skinned but instead to look for those treasured people with whom we feel naturally inspired, and with whom our gifts feel seen, appreciated, and cherished. These people are gold. They are the path to a future of intimacy and happiness. If we assume the 90 percent rule to be true, we will save ourselves from the gnawing self-doubt of thinking that we are too picky, or that there's something wrong with us.

You may ask, "If I follow the 90 percent rule do I have to resign myself to waiting almost forever? If so few people can match me in this way, doesn't that reduce my chances dramatically?"

My response is, "Not at all." When we know that we only want attractions of inspiration, and assume that most people won't meet that criterion, we move that much more quickly. We become wise warriors who don't waste time, because we only choose relationships where we feel inspiration. Follow the 90 percent rule and you'll save vast amounts of time—and avoid lots of heartbreak. When your primary dating goal becomes finding (and being!) an attraction of inspiration, not only will you be more likely to notice and value such people; you will also actually become increasingly attracted to them simply because they meet your new personal goal. In a 2008 study researchers Gráinne Fitzsimons and J. Y. Shah reported that we become more attracted to people who help us meet the goals that matter most to us. In addition, we notice and approach them more readily, and evaluate them more positively, while becoming less interested in those who do not help us meet our pressing personal goals.[4] In other words, simply committing to the personal goal of only choosing attractions of inspiration will make you notice those wonderful people more quickly, approach them more readily, and actually become more attracted to them. The reverse will happen with your attractions of deprivation.

Let's come back to Sandy, who owned a thriving Mexican restaurant in a suburb of New York. At work she was immersed in a constant social frenzy. When she came home, she felt alone—and although she knew she was too isolated, she liked it because it was safe. One of Sandy's Core Gifts was a deep sense of honesty. She told me that she kept herself apart because of a trait that she considered a weakness. "I've got a thing about honesty," she told me. "If I feel like someone isn't honest with me, something deep

inside of me completely shuts down. I think I must be too judgmental. Most people aren't honest enough for me. I feel like I'm
too fixated upon this honesty thing, and if I don't relax my standards, I'll avoid the world."

I told her about the 90 percent rule. And her first reaction was
like most people's: "How depressing. In that case, maybe I should
just give up!" I explained to her this way: "Imagine a hungry cus-
tomer in your restaurant who just doesn't know what they want to
eat. Now imagine someone who knows she wants a steak burrito.
Which order goes quickest?" And Sandy began to get it. She was
avoiding intimacy because her gift didn't feel safe in the world. To
feel safe in an intimate relationship, Sandy needed to be with one
of those rare and precious people who, like her, had an inner compass constitutionally pointed north, toward honesty.

I suggested that if she honored the value of her gift by becoming much more discriminating around this critical point, she would
become less afraid of intimacy. "And," I told her, "when you decide
to spend time with only those precious people who share your gift,
you're probably going to know a sense of happiness and peace that
you've been waiting for your whole life."

Sandy took this to heart. She began to follow the 90 percent
rule, and to live as if her honesty was a treasured gift. This changed
everything for her. She began to set better limits. When she dated,
she looked for people's ability to be honest even when it was hard.
And when she met these rare men, she recognized their worth.
Within six months she began dating Ed, who had been a regular at
her restaurant for years. Ed is a divorced father of three children.
He has the same gift of essential honesty, along with a sense of quiet
loyalty that she has come to trust and rely upon. They are engaged
to be married, and she feels like she's found a home in the world in
a way that she had despaired of ever finding.

I encourage you to make a commitment to yourself, right now.
Decide to choose only relationships and attractions of inspiration.
You may be thinking, *What a fairy tale. Finding someone like that is*

like finding a needle in a haystack. But I think you will be amazed by what happens when you only pursue attractions of inspiration. Our refusal to spend time and energy in dynamics of deprivation clears a space that gets filled with better relationships. We have the power to change our dating life—and our future—with this one simple and self-loving commitment.

Deeper Dating Workbook

PERSONAL EXERCISES
Developing an Eye for Inspiration

Think of one attribute of yours that would make you an attraction of inspiration to someone else. Who in your life taught you the most about becoming that kind of person? Remember back to a moment in which this person inspired or touched you by how he or she treated you or someone else. Take a few moments to remember and appreciate this person.

DEEPER DATING EXERCISES
Inspiration and Deprivation on a Date

Any time you are on a date or meet someone new, notice that person's qualities of inspiration or deprivation. Do you get a sense of warmth from this person? Do you feel a sense of integrity? Is this person thoughtful? Engaging? Can he listen and is he interested in you? Or does he keep speaking about himself? What is the quality of your connection like? These are all questions you can ask yourself. If you see qualities of inspiration, let yourself value that in this person. If you sense continuing qualities of deprivation over time, seriously consider moving on.

LEARNING PARTNER EXERCISES

Inspiration and Deprivation in Your Romantic History

1. Share two stories from your lives: one of an important attraction of inspiration and one of a significant attraction of deprivation.

2. Try the "Inspiration and Deprivation on a Date" exercise and share with your learning partner what you each learned and experienced on your date.

5

How Your Attractions Reveal Your Core Gifts

The type of human being we prefer reveals the contours of our heart.

—JOSÉ ORTEGA Y GASSET

In the last chapter I shared the simplest and most important principle of dating that I know: find—and then follow—*only* your attractions of inspiration. This choice is the foundation for your future of happiness in love. The more you recognize the specific characteristics of your own attractions of deprivation and inspiration, the more you will be able to consciously steer a course toward a truly wonderful relationship. In this chapter you will create a portrait of both of your types of attractions and discover the Core Gifts that lie within them.

HOW OUR ATTRACTIONS REVEAL OUR GIFTS

We can discover our Core Gifts and evaluate how much we honor them by looking at whom we are consistently drawn to. Within every attraction of deprivation is an unrecognized or undervalued Core Gift. For example, if we haven't learned how to honor our deep sensitivity, we will probably be attracted to people who diminish or degrade that sensitivity. If we haven't learned how to honor our gifts of passion and intensity, one of our most compelling attractions will be to people who ultimately try to deflate or criticize our passion. And if we haven't learned how to honor our longing for connection, the kind of partners we will be intensely attracted to will be people who resist commitment, push us away, or dishonor our need for closeness. It's almost as though our attractions of deprivation are the universe's way of saying, "There's work to be done around your relationship to this gift."

Fortunately, in each of these cases the reverse is also true. The more we learn to value those attributes in ourselves, the more we will find ourselves attracted to people who cherish those qualities in us and are careful not to abuse or take advantage of them.

Jung explained why this is so. He taught that when we repress a part of ourselves because we judge it harshly or feel ashamed or frightened of it, it turns into our "shadow"—an aspect of ourself that we try to bury. But the authentic self cannot be destroyed, and its power and energy need to go *somewhere*. So that denied part of us takes form in our external life as a "projection," a distorted and exaggerated version of the quality we tried to bury. When this happens, we continually find ourselves drawn to, or stuck with, people that act out this disowned part of ourselves in an exaggerated and negative way—and they often act it out on *us*! In dating, this means that if we deny or dishonor a Core Gift, we are likely to choose someone who also dishonors it—and then to be intensely vulnerable to any negative judgment they have about us. Our projections attack and dwarf us in the form of attractions of deprivation and unhealthy loves, until we reclaim the deep gifts we have rejected. When that happens, we gradually lose our magnetic attraction to people who ultimately denigrate those gifts.

When we embrace our gifts, they feed and enhance us. When we deny them, they haunt us, often through relationships that demean that exact part of ourselves.

This proposition leads us to a key insight: at the heart of every attraction, no matter how unhealthy, lies a gift—a deep part of ourselves looking for expression, gratification, connection, and validation. I encourage you to honor the gift at the heart of every one of your attractions, even the ones that you know are bad for you. At the heart of our longing for love, however misguided, lies our soul. If we can feel an attraction and sense the gift that lies below it, we are much more likely to make wise choices in relation to that attraction.

As you do the exercises in this chapter, you will come face to face with many of your own attractions. Some of them will be inspiring and beautiful. Some may feel troubling. At such times it's important to remember two things. First, don't be quick to pathologize your attractions. Many of us have attractions that others might judge as confusing or unacceptable, or that we feel uncomfortable with. If it's an attraction of inspiration, causes no harm, brings joy, and is mutual, then it deserves to be explored, not resisted according to some cultural bias of appropriate relationships. Instead of beginning with a cold judgment of such an attraction, instead try honoring the richness it may have to offer you.

Second, remember a central tenet of Gift Theory: your deepest wounds spring from your greatest gifts. Once you identify the gifts behind your unhealthy attractions, you have the beginnings of a path toward healing. *You can't deconstruct negative behaviors if you don't rescue the gift within them and guide it to something better.*

The Myth of Lost Love

Our attractions of deprivation are fueled by lack of self-love, but this link between our unhealthy attractions and our lack of self-love is not immediately obvious to most of us. We need a deeper understanding of how our unconscious self-rejection turns into unhealthy attraction. Becoming aware of our "myth of lost love" can make this connection clearer. Each of us has created a myth of lost love, a life-defining story we use to explain why we weren't loved the way we needed to be when we were children and what we can do to repair that pain, or to protect ourselves from experiencing it again. This myth comes alive for us when we feel unsafe in a relationship, and it can stir us to our very core. Debbie offers a good example of how our myth of lost love can play out in our intimate relationships.

Debbie fought often with her boyfriends. No relationships seemed to last. One or both partners would become too battle-scarred to continue. At one point in therapy Debbie brought in a memory from her childhood. When she was about four years old she found a dead monarch butterfly lying on the pavement. It broke her heart to confront the reality of death in something so beautiful. Crying, she picked up the butterfly and held it out to her aunt, who was standing on the porch. Her aunt looked at Debbie's tear-stained face and began to laugh uproariously. Furious, Debbie dropped the butterfly and hauled off and slugged her aunt! In the past, Debbie had only seen this as a funny, slightly embarrassing memory, but now it gave her the key to understanding an important part of her relationship history.

As she described her childlike fury, she finally recognized the message in this memory. It was about her tender heart—and the passionate fury that surfaced when her vulnerability was spurned. For the first time she was able to embrace her warriorlike feistiness and her soft heart at the same time. Seeing both parts of herself so clearly, she began to cry, but now her tears were mixed with under-standing laughter. Her hair-trigger temper finally began to make sense. Every time her soul felt unrecognized, her anger flared—and got her into trouble.

The myth of lost love has three main aspects. The first is the story we tell ourselves as children about the ways in which the world is an unsafe and unloving place. Debbie's father divorced her mother when Debbie was just seven years old. Being a single parent with four older boys and one sensitive little girl to raise, Debbie's mother had little time or energy for her. Her mother seemed angry all the time. Debbie's attempts to show love to her mother were sometimes returned, but at other times they were rebuffed or ig-nored completely. Debbie only remembered a few times when her mother had shown her real affection. At times, her mother would even humiliate Debbie when she showed her soft side. As a result, Debbie grew up experiencing the world as a cold place where real love was mostly unattainable. Unconsciously she developed her own myth of lost love to explain why her mother's love was being denied her. She came to the conclusion that the world was a cold place that rewarded need and vulnerability with humiliation.

Second, the myth of lost love explains that we *deserve* this punishment. As a child Debbie had no way of knowing that her mother was the problem. She loved her mother and so she explained her mother's limitations in the way that makes sense to a child. "It's my fault. I'm just unlovable. I just *need too much,* and people hate that." Debbie grew up feeling that somehow *she* was the reason that real love was unattainable. Our myth of lost love continues its path of damage by telling us exactly what makes us unworthy of love. Debbie's myth explained what was wrong with her in the most crippling terms. It homed in on her most vulnerable, needy qualities, and on the qualities that were most ignored or misunderstood—her Core Gifts of tenderness and passionate emotionality—and convinced her that those gifts were to blame for her loss of love. It taught her that her vulnerability and intensity were humiliating traits that made her unlovable. Because her vulnerability was shamed instead of loved, she was simply unable to experience it as a good thing.

Third, our myth of lost love instructs us in how to protect and defend ourselves in an unsafe world. As a child Debbie learned to be quiet in the face of her mother's anger. She tried to be the best little girl in the world. But the anger that took root in Debbie as a child came to full bloom in Debbie as an adult. Although she was still trying to be the best little girl in the world, she also vowed never to be humiliated again. Instead, whenever she felt vulnerable, whenever she even felt *afraid* of being unloved, she would mount a preemptive strike. Her sudden, over-the-top anger continually undermined and eventually destroyed each new budding relationship.

As an adult Debbie had learned to despise the gifts at the core of her identity. She believed, quite wrongly, that her vulnerability, her tenderness, and her sensitivity were weaknesses that she needed to overcome. In fact, they were signposts pointing to Debbie's Core Gifts, so all her efforts to overcome or suppress them ultimately failed. Those gifts—her vulnerability and fiery nature—were a central part of Debbie's very being. As hard as she tried to get far away from them, an invisible string always kept her attached. At a certain point, the string just stopped stretching. She realized that she hadn't found the love she wanted, that the life she had dreamed of was passing her by. She felt an inexplicable emptiness inside—and she didn't know what to do about it.

In therapy Debbie discovered that by suppressing her Core Gifts she was rejecting her very being. As we talked she discovered an important similarity among almost all of her past boyfriends: none of them was comfortable with her vulnerability or with his own. In fact, they all made her feel *ashamed* of her vulnerability. Now she had the blueprint behind her attractions of deprivation. She saw that her most intense but unhealthy attractions were to people who couldn't appreciate her Core Gifts, people who (like Debbie herself) were unable to value vulnerability, tenderness, or sensitivity.

She realized that the pain she had felt in past relationships *was the pain of a gift that had never been loved into fullness.* She had wasted years of her life trying to get someone who was as judgmental toward her Core Gifts as *she* was to love and approve of her. Finally she realized that suppressing her Core Gifts would never let her obtain the genuine intimacy she desired. Debbie's task at that point was to follow that invisible string back to the gifts she had left behind, to identify them, cherish them, and to let them lead her to a man who could also recognize and treasure her gifts. That kind of man would be her attraction of inspiration.

Now her powerful will lined up behind a new goal: this was the only kind of man she would settle for. He didn't have to be perfectly comfortable with vulnerability; God knows, *she* wasn't—but he had to be someone who would never knowingly make her feel ashamed of hers. Now she began to evaluate the people she dated on the basis of this new criterion. As she began to surround herself with people who valued her vulnerability, she slowly began to experience it in a new way: as something tender, yet still strong and worthy. This new sense of discrimination and self-awareness changed the tenor of her entire dating life—quickly!

LEARNING FROM YOUR ATTRACTIONS OF DEPRIVATION

The next process, creating a clear portrait of your attractions of deprivation, will help you identify the negative and withholding qualities that keep drawing you in. As a result of this process, you will also be able to identify the gifts you need to honor more fully. Go through this process and discuss it with your learning partner. But be aware that this exercise involves the reliving of some painful memories. If you have experienced trauma or abuse in past relationships, if you are newly sober, or if you have any reason to think that this process might be destabilizing for you, I strongly advise you to do it only with the support of a qualified psychotherapist.

Also, please note that the purpose of this process is not to bash your exes. It is to use a particular filter to discover your Core Gifts.

Unveiling Your Attractions of Deprivation

1. Working in your journal, set aside five consecutive pages for this process. On the top of the first page, write "My Attractions of Deprivation." Write a list of the names of the important loves from your past that left you feeling hurt, deprived, neglected, or betrayed. If some relationships had inspiring *and* depriving aspects, name that person and only write down their deprivational attributes. Leave a few lines for each name. If you wish, feel free to include important non-romantic relationships including those from your childhood.

2. For each person, list every trait that hurt you, upset you, or made you feel unseen or unacknowledged. Don't worry if the fault might have been partly yours. Write the trait down anyway. Include physical traits and personality traits that felt sexy but also negative, like a cuttingly sharp wit, a cocky swagger, or a tight, angry mouth.

3. This next step is very strong medicine: Ask your closest friends how they would characterize your relationships of deprivation (the kind of people you choose who treat you or others poorly). Add those negative aspects to your list.

Our friends can usually see the deprivation part of our relationships—even when we're lost in the attraction part. Let your friends be the mirror that helps you through your blind spots around your attractions of deprivation. If you think you are not ready to hear a friend's feedback or if you feel it will cause you undue shame or make you angry at that friend, don't do this step. Otherwise: Do. Not. Skip. It. Our closest friends can tell us in a New York minute how we block ourselves from finding real love. But do we ask? And do we listen? Now is your chance to learn something very important about the patterns that keep you from love.

4. On the second page, write "My Patterns of Deprivation." Look at the full list of people and their deprivational qualities. Pick the negative traits that hurt you *most deeply* or *most frequently* in your romantic history. Note who had this trait. For example, let's look at Dana's answer to this question:

Resentful of my success (James, Brad, David, Rob)

Cocky, arrogant (James, Peter, Brad, Steven)

Drank too much (James, David, Rob, Brad)

Mean streak (James, Peter, Steven, Rob)

Cheated on me (Brad)

Isolating the traits that have hurt you most deeply and/or occurred the most frequently will enable you to find the central qualities of your attractions of deprivation. If you don't have enough romantic experience to answer these questions, look at your nonromantic relationships and use those.

5. On top of the third page, write "A Profile of My Attractions of Deprivation." Read through your list, including your friends' feedback, and put together a profile of the types of people who draw you in and their traits that cause you the most pain.

    For example, Dana wrote: "I'm attracted to bad boys. Guys who have no problem expressing their anger or their needs, who aren't afraid of a fight. James had a mean streak that came out with me and with his mom. Angry people. Guys who don't need me like I need them. Guys who don't need the validation I need. A lot of them drank too much. Brad cheated on me over a period of a few months. It was probably the worst experience of my life. All of them were sexy in their bravado. My friends experienced a lot of them as really arrogant, especially Brad, which I never even realized! Most were less successful in their professional life than I was. Most resented my successes. They were critical of me, and I ended up feeling guilty a lot of the time. I'm attracted to guys who have a sort of disdainful look on their face. Guys in the street who are surly and even a little dangerous turn me on."

6. On the top of the fourth page, write "How I Felt in These Relationships." Write your answer to this question: What impact did these relationships have on your sense of self? Describe the feelings they evoke.

    For example: "I feel small. Weak. Diminished. Unsure of myself. And that makes me incredibly angry. I hate feeling weak. I don't want to show how angry I am because I'm afraid they will leave me. I feel guilty—as though I am responsible for their frustration and anger. At the same time, I feel love. I want to help them. And at the same time as I desire them, I want to knock them down to size."

7. Finally, on top of the fifth page, write "The Core Gifts Beneath My Attractions of Deprivation." Your answers to question 6 captured the unique wounds that surround your Core Gifts. In this step you will identify the Core Gifts that were dishonored in these relationships. Those are the parts of your most essential self that you haven't learned to treasure. The more you name them, understand them, and value them, the less you will be susceptible to these attractions of deprivation in the future and the more you will be drawn to your attractions of inspiration.

Here are two insights that will help you to discover your Core Gifts in the heart of your attractions of deprivation.

Insight 1: Often, the negative qualities you keep finding in your relationships are the exact opposite attributes of a Core Gift you haven't learned to honor. For example, one of Dana's Core Gifts was her competence and ambition, but she felt ashamed and guilty about her power. Therefore, her attractions of deprivation were to unsuccessful, self-sabotaging men—the exact opposite qualities of her Core Gift.

Which negative traits were most common or most painful in your exes? Think of the positive opposite quality. Describe that quality as a Core Gift you haven't learned to embrace.

Insight 2: The most painful feelings you experience in an attraction of deprivation reflect a Core Gift that has never been "loved into fullness." When we have a Core Gift that has not been acknowledged, respected, or valued in our life, we experience feelings of pain and inadequacy when we are in touch with that gift. When that gift is honored, we begin to experience it not as a deficit but as something positive, and it grows slowly stronger. For example, in the exercise above, Dana described feeling weak and unsure of herself, even though she was effective and successful. Her innate power, never honored or loved into fullness, was experienced as inadequacy. As she learns to choose friends and a future mate who enjoy her innate power, she will gradually begin to experience that power as a Core Gift.

Choose one feeling that was most painful or most pervasive in your past attractions of deprivation. Describe that painful feeling as a gift that was never loved into fullness.

If you are not yet clear on the gifts that lie below these attractions, give it time. These are complex and new concepts. As you discover your gifts in other areas, the gifts beneath your attractions of deprivation will become clearer.

Take a few minutes to read what you wrote, and notice your feelings as you let it sink in. Try not to judge yourself; this painful knowledge is exactly what will set you free you from future replays. Now you have a much clearer picture of the specific traits of your attractions of deprivation—a veritable checklist of your personal "warning signs." The next time you notice these traits in someone you date, you'll be more aware, more self-honoring, and more likely to make a wise choice. Congratulations on having just completed one of the hardest exercises in this book!

DISCOVERING YOUR GIFTS IN ATTRACTIONS OF INSPIRATION

For some of us, attractions of inspiration are simply not familiar. We're used to the pain of longing, the thrill of the chase, the familiar

feeling of desire mixed with uncertainty. Many of us need to cultivate a taste for inspiration, peace, and consistency. This doesn't
mean that the relationship has to be boring. Relationships that
are inspiring can have a wonderful "edge," but that edge comes
from being able to express differences and reveal new levels of
passion, enthusiasm, vulnerability, and sexual adventurousness.
Excitement and thrill can exist in healthy relationships. They just
don't usually feel like the thrill in unhealthy relationships. As we
cultivate our capacity for real intimacy we become much more
likely to notice and pursue our attractions of inspiration.

My father is a Holocaust survivor. He was a sensitive kid with a
wild streak. He would read poetry in bed under the covers at night,
but that was a secret none of his peers would ever find out. He was
deeply close to his mother, who was a loving and kind single mom.
When the Nazis came, they put them both into the same concentration camp but separated them. This was the last time he ever saw
his mother. He was sixteen years old. After surviving years of horror,
when the Allied forces liberated their concentration camp, my father immediately began to search for his mother. They had agreed
to meet in a particular town if either or both of them survived. He
went there, and waited for her for months, until he realized that she
must have perished.

When he knew there was no hope left of finding her he moved
to the United States. Just a few years later he met my mother. Her
goodness and care touched the same part of his soul that his mother
had touched, and in her, he knew he had found his home in the
world. My mother was smitten by him too; he was the kind of person who was always there when anyone had a problem. If there was
a job to be done, you could count on Eric to do it. My father
knew—he just knew—that she was for him. So after three dates he
proposed to her. She was nineteen at the time, and terrified. She
fled back to her home in Chicago to get her bearings. My father
waited—and waited. She had become his lifeline to the possibility
of a good and happy life. She represented things that he had shut
his heart to for years but that he now realized he wanted and needed

more than anything. He wrote her one raw, simple letter. In that letter, he essentially pleaded with her to marry him. At this point in my father's life, he didn't let *anyone* see his vulnerability. I can only imagine what it cost him to write that letter. Yet that letter changed the course of both their lives. Her heart went out to him. In the emotional turmoil she experienced in response to his plea, she realized that she loved him, and she said yes. Just nineteen, a bohemian artist just beginning to explore the world, she still knew that she had to say yes to a future with my father. They are in their eighties now, and they still have one of the most loving and powerful relationships I've ever seen.

My father tells the story now of how frightened he was to love again. His deepest fear was to fall in love and to have a family, because, in his words, "When you love, the world can hold you hostage." When he fell in love with my mother, he made the most frightening choice possible: to love, and hence to risk, once again.

My mother also told me a wonderful story. When she began to see my father, she was dating another man who really liked her. One day it became clear whom she would continue dating. She and the other fellow were sitting on a park bench. He had gotten a bag of chips—only one bag. He ate from the bag first, and then offered her some. She pictured my father, and she knew he would have brought *two bags*, or if he only had one, he would have offered it first to her. In that brief moment she imagined two different versions of her future—and she knew the future she wanted.

Both my father and mother were struck by inspiration, by the goodness in each other. And both of them realized that following inspiration was the path to happiness—even though, in their own ways, they were frightened by what that choice would mean for them. Through countless problems and struggles, that bedrock of respect for the other's goodness is what kept them together and in love for all these years.

In the next section you'll learn how to recognize the hallmarks of your own attractions of inspiration.

Unveiling Your Attractions of Inspiration

1. Working in your journal, set aside three consecutive pages for this process. At the top of the first page, write "My Attractions of Inspiration." List every romantic relationship that had an inspirational element. If some relationships also had deprivational aspects, include that person's name anyway. Leave a few lines for each name.

2. After each name list all the traits of your exes that inspired you, touched you, and moved you. Don't worry if these qualities also had dark sides. Just write down the good parts. Include physical traits that were attractive because they were inspiring; for example, laughing eyes, a kind mouth, and so on. If, in the course of this exercise, you notice feelings of nostalgia, love, or regret, allow those feelings to arise and see if you can feel gratitude toward your exes for their qualities of inspiration.

3. On the top of the second page, write "A Portrait of My Attractions of Inspiration." Refer back to the list you just wrote and begin to put together a profile of the qualities that inspired you in these relationships. Write from the heart, and let yourself enjoy the process.

    For example: "I've always been attracted to men who are brave enough to speak and live their truth, even when that's hard to do. Maybe that's the most important quality of all. I really need someone who treasures family. When I'm with someone and I know his loyalty runs deep, I begin to let go and trust. Kindness means a lot to me. When I see a man being kind to strangers, doing volunteer work, or having a degree of patience with kids I don't think I'll ever have, it moves me greatly. I love being with someone who can share deeply and honestly, even about the hard stuff. When I am with someone to whom I can tell the truth, and he won't flee me, my heart melts. A man who really gives himself in bed, who lets me feel his passion but also his need—that just kills me."

4. Take a breath. Read what you wrote and let it enter into you. Now, allow yourself to envision being in a relationship with an available person who has these qualities. The more vivid your picture, the more you'll long for it, and the more you'll do to make it come true.

5. On the top of the third page, write "My Core Gifts." Look at the qualities of inspiration you listed in step three. Now, see which of those also describes you. I imagine that a number of them do, because that is why they touch you so deeply in another person. In most cases, these will be gifts that you are not ashamed of, gifts that you allow yourself to honor. Write down these qualities and let yourself appreciate the work, time, and cost of having cultivated these gifts in the world.

For example: "Honesty matters so deeply to me. That is a powerful Core Gift, and God knows I've been hurt enough and bewildered enough by being in relationships with men who just didn't value truth the way I do. I also am not someone who hides my emotional truth. I share it. And I don't jump ship. So many men I've dated haven't shared what was upsetting them in the relationship and left me with almost no explanation. I would never, never do that to someone. This is an incredible gift, and I see now, a very rare one."

Now that you know some of the traits of your attractions of inspiration, you can look for them in a focused way, and that will ignite wonderful changes in your search for love.

If this chapter made you think of old attractions of inspiration that you might not have been able to appreciate in the past, perhaps one of those people might be single and available. There's no shame in contacting them again. You might acknowledge your past fear when you reach out to them. And they might become a friend—or maybe even more.

Deeper Dating Workbook

PERSONAL EXERCISE

Becoming Someone Else's Attraction of Inspiration

What might you do to become more of an attraction of inspiration for the people you date? Pick one behavior that would feel good to develop. Share it with your learning partner, try it on your next date or in any interaction, and report back about your experience.

LEARNING PARTNER EXERCISE

Your Attractions of Deprivation and Inspiration

Discuss the results of your work with the attractions of inspiration and attractions of deprivation exercises. Describe as clearly as possible the attributes of your "type" when it comes to attractions of deprivation and inspiration.

6

Tapping Your
Deepest Roots

How Five Minutes a Day Can Change Your Life

Behold, a sacred voice is calling you; All over the sky a sacred voice is calling.

—BLACK ELK

If our goal is to find love, then we would be wise to start with our connection to the very *source* of that love inside us. When we come close to that source, we feel the presence of something greater, something with tremendous untapped promise. Our Core Gifts—the places where we feel our humanity most deeply—are our personal access points to this Source of Self. They are where we feel the most connection to the world and to others. They are where our spirit yearns to interact with the world.

In this chapter you will learn techniques to help you ally with your own source of wisdom, creativity, and love as you search for your beloved. In the end spirituality and intimacy are one and the same: love is the final goal. There is no need to believe in any kind of deity to follow the lessons of this chapter. You can simply think of the source from which your love and your deepest gifts spring.

We can think of our Core Gifts as being shards of that vast source within us—shards that have their origin in a vastness, depth, and humanity that is bigger than our minds can picture. And that's why they get us into so much trouble. Imagine having a piece of something so deep, so tender, so unimaginably vast inside a person who's fragile and self-involved, living inside a small and limited body that will age and die. As you might well imagine, such a scenario can lead to great suffering and to great beauty—which sounds very much like the human experience. Our gifts will always be larger than we are. They arise from a source that's far deeper than our best thinking can ever touch.

MICRO-MEDITATION

Your Source of Self | Three minutes

Have you ever had a moment in life so beautiful that you might call it transcendent or sacred? Perhaps it was a moment in nature, or a spiritual experience, a deep feeling of love, or a profound experience listening to music. Whatever it was, remember it to the best of your ability. Be light with yourself; simply revisiting the memory is enough. Try to remember where you were when it happened and what it felt like. This was a moment when you were close to your Source of Self. If there was a message for you in that experience, what might that be? Hold your memory close for another moment. Take a breath in, and feel the ripples.

GUIDING INSIGHTS: YOUR GPS TO A LIFE OF LOVE AND MEANING

Buried in all the nagging "shoulds" of self-improvement lie our Guiding Insights: messages from our deepest self that have the power to change our lives.

Guiding Insights compel us; they feel like marching orders from our deepest self. They call to us when our guard is down.

Have you ever woken up at 3 A.M. to a moment of stark insight about your life? Or listened to a piece of music and felt a rush of love or an intense sense of connection to someone important in your life? Mark's experience of being shaken awake in the night was a life-changing Guiding Insight for him. As you spend more time in the warm humanity of your Gift Zone, you can expect to be visited by these almost magical allies.

Guiding Insights hit you where you live. They may challenge you or soothe you, but they touch your heart. You know that they matter. They may make your heart ache (that very ache is often a sign of a Guiding Insight). They may feel like liberation or like a comforting caress. Or they may scare the hell out of you. They may be undefined, embryonic, forming even while you're feeling your way into them. But if they don't have a deep sense of resonance for you, they are not your Guiding Insights—no matter how practical they are. Guiding Insights won't tell you your future mate's home address (unless you're very lucky!). They may even feel unrelated to your dating life. Yet they mysteriously lead you to love. Your job is to invite them, welcome them when they arrive, and try to act on the messages they send you.

The intimacy-based search for love is more like a treasure hunt than a car trip to an exact location. In a treasure hunt, your instructions only reveal your next step: "Walk two blocks west and look under the mailbox to find your next clue." If you want to continue the journey, you must simply act on that clue. Your Guiding Insights are like a clue on a treasure hunt. They don't give you the final answer; they just offer you a glimpse of your next step. When you honor that message, it will *take* you somewhere, and then in time another message will come.

However, Guiding Insights rarely come in a form as clear as the note in a treasure hunt. They come in whispers, a moment when life priorities become clear: feeling an attraction of inspiration toward someone you hadn't really noticed before, an insight that rescues you from a painful predicament, a fresh sense of treasuring someone you love. Those whispers are personal invitations to intimacy from our inner self. When you hear them, honor them. Write them down. Every now and then, ask to be shown your Guiding Insights. When you start this process, new insights will begin to arise more frequently in unexpected moments of your daily life. If you let them, they will guide your intimacy journey more and more. In time a picture will begin to emerge of your own path to love and growth. If you're willing to honor the Guiding Insights in your life, your dating life will change, and you'll feel a new sense of comfort and connection, knowing that you are less alone in your search for love than you might ever have imagined.

MICRO-MEDITATION

Inviting Your Guiding Insights | Four minutes

This gentle yet powerful micro-meditation will help you learn to tune in to your own guiding insights. Just ask yourself this question, "Right now, what is love asking of me?" Take a few moments to settle into this question and to notice what answers come up. Your answer may be nonspecific or unclear. It may be surprising. But if it has a ring of "rightness" for you, let yourself claim it. Think about how you might act on it. Take one more moment to just rest with whatever "whisper" came to you. If nothing came, try it again at another point in your day. (This micro-meditation can also be incredibly helpful during a conflict, because it creates a "reset" and moves you into the warmth and creativity of your Gift Zone.)

Do this process as many times as you wish. Try not to second-guess yourself. You're learning a new language of intuition.

Following the Call of Your Guiding Insights

When I was forty-four, I saw Pedro Almodóvar's brilliant film, *All about My Mother*. A central theme of this movie concerns the power of caring for others. After the movie I felt an odd sensation inside. I had no idea what it was. I walked to a quiet part of the theater lobby and closed my eyes. What was I feeling? After about a minute this tug inside me became clear.

I wanted to become a dad. I was a single gay man in my forties and by no means wealthy, but I was certain that I was being called to fatherhood. About one year later I brought my baby son home from Cambodia and we became a family. Creating a family has been the greatest, most joyful blessing of my entire life. I worried that the demands of being a single dad would keep me from finding love, but in fact, the opposite happened. I met my wonderful partner, Greg, who is also a dad, through an event for our children.

As you follow your Guiding Insights your life will unfold in surprising ways and you'll spend more time living in your Gift Zone. If you act on these lessons, you will become more creative. You'll have less tolerance for relationships of deprivation and you'll become more attracted to relationships of inspiration. You'll become a better friend to yourself and your loved ones. These are not empty promises, and this is no secret formula. Our hearts are whispering to us—sometimes shouting to us—all the time. The issue isn't that we're not being called; it's that we prefer to ignore that call.

And here's an amazing bonus: the more you follow your Guiding Insights, the more attractive you'll become—to the kind of person you're really looking for. The more you follow the calls of your heart, the more you'll find that the kind of person you date will actually begin to change.

Loving the Lesson

Sometimes we're not ready to answer the call of our Guiding Insights. When we are not ready to act, a wise thing to do is to simply love the lesson, knowing we can't act on it yet. Little by little the very proximity to our lesson changes us, creates a friction inside us,

a noticeable *discomfort* that slowly transforms us. Just loving a lesson changes us and moves us closer to the day we can act on it.

For example, let's say one of your Guiding Insights is that you
need to slow down, that you're so focused on your next tasks and
issues that the important moments and relationships in your life are
passing you by. Yet you don't have the strength or capacity to slow
down the merry-go-round of your life. Instead of berating yourself,
or thinking you'll come back to this problem when you're stronger
or wiser (as most of us think we need to do), try something else instead. Love the voice that's telling you to slow down. Think about
its wisdom. Think about your sadness at your missed moments with
loved ones. Instead of avoiding that discomfort, allow it to live in
you. Over time, that insight will change you, because it will become impossible to live in the old way while your inner self is prod-
ding you—through your own discomfort—to change.

TAPPING INTO YOUR SOURCE OF SELF

The exercise I'm going to teach you now may make more difference in your dating life than any other single thing, outside of a
great learning partner. It involves tapping into your Source of Self
for guidance and inspiration in your search for love. This Source is
the place that you love *from*. Here is a simple exercise to help you
move closer to it: Ask yourself, "Do I find a kind of gravitational pull
toward intimacy inside myself?" (Of course you do!)

Now imagine following that gravitational pull deep down to
its source inside you, as if you were holding on to a rope and following it inward. Imagine following that rope deep into your core,
toward the power and love that lie in your Source of Self, toward
the living spring of your own goodness. That spring is something
you can tap into.

When we access that spring in the core of our being, we feel the
presence of something greater, something with tremendous, positive promise. We don't have to name it. Simply loving it and spending "quality time" with it are enough to change us. The closer we

come to it, the more we meet it skin to skin, the more quality time we spend with it, the more our life will be transformed, simplified, and inspired. The greater our intimacy with this source, the more the frozen parts of our heart will begin to thaw. And then love, and its twin, the longing for love, will begin to emerge in our life. In my opinion, that is the true spiritual path.

The couples therapist and author David E. Greenan has written, "Believers, agnostics, and atheists all recognize the power of connection; the peace and calm that comes from opening your heart to another. In those moments, we know we're in the presence of something that inspires awe; something synergistically bigger than ourselves."[1]

Let's create a personal practice that enlists the aid of this mysterious, benevolent force in your journey to love.

Your Five-Minute Meditation on Love

Find a place where you feel safe and peaceful. Sit down in this spot with a pen and paper. Think about the place you want to connect with, the source of your love. You might or might not have a name for it: the great mystery, your untapped potential, a higher power — all of those are fine.

Now see if you can create words that ask for help in your search for your loved one. Find the words that speak of your desire or longing for love. You might ask for help and direction in finding your soul mate. You might ask for help in learning not to run from love. Be brave and use the words that grab you, that ignite your longing. Also, feel free to use words, affirmations, and prayers you've read or heard that hit home for you. They can be a phrase, a word, or a few sentences. *The only requirement is that the words move you or touch your heart when you say or think them.* Try your words on for size. If you need to, refine them to the point where they really hit home. Don't worry about sounding wise or polished. Just the words *help me* are enough.

Write these words down. You will use them in your first

five-minute practice, but you're not stuck with those words forever. They can change many times, based upon what you feel—even in the course of one five-minute period! From now on, you can use these words as often as you like, or find new ones before you do your practice, or just create the words of your desire anew each time.

If you prefer to use an affirmation, that is fine as well. Create or find a sentence that feels hopeful, believable, and moving. For example, you might picture your next partner and repeat, "My love, I open my heart to you." You will know if an affirmation is correct if it rings true to you *and* moves you.

Once you've selected your words or affirmation, get comfortable in whichever place you have chosen. Allow yourself to imagine the Source of Love inside you. Don't worry about getting it right. Just imagining it imperfectly is more than enough.

Say the words you have chosen, putting your heart into that process. Rest a moment and feel the ripples inside you. Now say the same words again, and take another moment to feel the emotional ripples. Don't worry if no feelings come up. It takes time to "prime the pump."

Continue doing this—saying the words from your heart and then taking a moment to feel whatever comes up after each repetition. Sometimes you'll find that a wave of feeling comes to you. You may feel longing, sadness, or joy. Whatever you are feeling is coming from deep within, and it is a sign that something is opening up inside. Take all the time for that wave of feeling to move through you. In those moments something is happening that can transform and guide us. It is as if a download is occurring, subtly changing our circuitry. Let the download complete and feel its ripples afterward.

When that wave of feeling passes and completes, go back to repeating the words again. Keep doing this gentle but oh-so-powerful process. After five minutes just rest and open to what you are feeling.

When we ask for what we most want in a repeated way, using the inner language of our personal yearning, we generate heat, emotion, and longing. Our fears may arise. We may sense that we don't deserve our heart's desire. We may begin to dread that it will never come. These are hard things to tolerate. Or we might acutely feel our longing, our passionate need and desire for partnership and family. That longing hurts too.

So why do something that might hurt, even for five minutes? Because *it works*. It changes our lives. It changes our characters and our behaviors. It sets forces in motion that are below the conscious mind. It aligns us with our desires. It pushes aside our protective layers of numbness, distractedness, and fixation on minor concerns.

This brief meditation reminds us of what we care about most. It saves us from getting lost in the relatively meaningless but hugely compelling dramas that fill our days. As we develop in our spiritual practice, our hearts begin to thaw and our longing for love is released. When that happens, a door opens up. We begin to get clearer messages of guidance. These Guiding Insights are our next steps and they tell us the very next things we need to do to embrace and discover love.

Make this process as authentic and creative as possible. Any method that helps you connect to your Source of Self to support your search for love is wonderful. I know someone who went into her yard every night before bed, looked at the sky, and thought about the fact that someone was out there, somewhere in the world, also lonely, looking for a person like her—they just hadn't found each other yet. Picturing that person, inviting him into her life, she would sing, "Goodnight My Someone," from *The Music Man*. Today, she attributes meeting her husband in part to those nights of quiet singing in her backyard.

Perhaps instead of asking, you prefer to practice trusting. Arielle Ford, the author of *The Soulmate Secret*, created a wonderful technique that she used to help her find her beloved. Prior to meeting her soul mate, Brian, she wrote, "I had a ritual feelingization: each day at sunset I would light several candles, put on my favorite CD of Gregorian chants, and sit in my big cozy chair. With my eyes closed, I would drop into the feeling of joy of having my soul mate in my life. I would experience these wonderful feelings in every part of my body, knowing that even at that moment he was on the way to me. There were days when the thought that he was very late did cross my mind, but I would just let those thoughts go and get back to feeling myself in a state of grace and knowing that his arrival was assured."[2]

Again, there is only one requirement for the practice you choose: that it touches and moves you. If you try a practice a few times and find this isn't happening at all, then try finding new words or creating a different practice.

Try to set aside five minutes every single day for your practice. You might even create a special place in your home for it.

In Praise of Sloppy Spiritual Practice

Doing an exercise like the above, even for five minutes, can be demanding—and immensely rewarding. My advice is to let yourself do it *badly*. Don't worry if your focus wanders. If your heart is in the process, even for moments, you will begin to experience change.

I am a great example of sloppy spiritual practice. What does that mean? My mind wanders. I lose interest. I spend much of my time making lists or rehashing grievances. I have been a sloppy—and consistent—practitioner of meditation for about twenty-five years. And yet, even with my terrible form, my unabashed sloppiness, my meditation life is rich beyond what I could have imagined. Meditation is like a gentle, wise presence inside my own heart. Why? Because I have been meditating *badly* for so many years!

Let the practice change as it wishes to change. Don't try to control it. Let it take on a life of its own. Sometimes it might feel completely dry and forced. Expect that. Yet sometimes it will touch you and your longing will be ignited. Or you might feel a sense of peace or hope. When that happens, you are in your Gift Zone. Stay with it. Keep your heart there, even if the longing hurts. The wave will pass. Enjoy those moments when, without warning, meditation takes wing. And it will. It might take weeks for this to happen or it might happen on the very first try. But whatever happens, I challenge you to try this practice every day throughout your whole work with this book, and thereafter. It will change your life.

Deeper Dating Workbook

PERSONAL EXERCISE
*Create and Begin to Practice Your
Five-Minute Meditation on Love*

Do this life-changing process every day for five minutes throughout the rest of this course—and hopefully thereafter. If you can't do five minutes, do three or two. Even that will make a difference. And of course if you want to take longer than five minutes, that's wonderful. This process will take on a life of its own, and you will see the changes that occur in your life as a result.

DEEPER DATING EXERCISE
Asking for a Guiding Insight

At any point in the day when you can concentrate, ask for a Guiding Insight about your dating life. Listen for any "whispers," any sense of a Guiding Insight, now and in the coming days. When and if you get a Guiding Insight, write it down. Then be sure to take the action your insight suggests. Your intuition will come forth more freely when you honor it by listening and acting on its guidance.

LEARNING PARTNER EXERCISES
Your Guiding Insights

Share your Guiding Insights with your learning partner and your loved ones. Their responses will help you understand your Guiding Insights in new ways, and translate them into new behaviors.

Your Five-Minute Practice

To the extent that it feels comfortable, share your experiences with your learning partner. The area of spirituality is a very tender one. It can be harder to talk about spirituality than about sex—especially if your spirituality doesn't fall into any easy categories. Don't share anything that doesn't feel ripe to share. At the least, mutually support each other in creating and following through on both of your practices, even if you don't go into specifics about the actual practice.

Learn the Skills
of Deeper Dating

In the first two stages of this book, you've done invaluable work in discovering your Core Gifts and understanding how they have influenced your entire relationship history. In this stage you will learn to bring the depth and beauty of your Core Gifts right into your dating life. Welcome to Stage 3, where you will use the tools of Deeper Dating to transform your quest for a loving and lasting relationship.

In this stage, you'll create a set of new dating tools that will allow you to share your truest self with kindness, bravery, and discrimination. You'll also learn where to look for love and what to do when you get there. In this most concrete stage in your journey, you'll learn to navigate through the difficult middle stage of the search for love, chart your progress, and discover your "Next Brave Step." Of tremendous importance, you'll also learn about the greatest saboteurs of new and healthy love and how to navigate their treacherous waters.

The Old Map to Love

Playing hard to get makes you more desirable to a new romantic interest. Showing your enthusiasm too soon will make that person flee.

The New Map to Love

Playing hard to get might be a good way to temporarily hook someone who is uncomfortable with intimacy—if that's what you're looking for. The myth that we should play it cool has kept many a potential relationship from being born. Most of us err on the side of believing we have to play it cool. The truth is, if you're too good at playing it cool, that's probably the sign of a problem. And if you're not skilled in this art, you'll probably "white-knuckle" your desire until you can't hold it in any longer, and then let it all out at the moment you'd least want to. (How many times has this happened to me!)

No, the research is quite clear on this: showing someone you're interested is one of the best ways to spark attraction. Eli Finkel, a professor of psychology at Northwestern University, used speed-dating events as a vehicle to study romantic attraction. His research showed that playing hard to get is not the way to go. A key to sparking romantic attraction is to show someone that you're interested in him in particular, not because of a generalized sense of need on your part. For example, Finkel suggests that you might convey the message "You are awesome, and I am so excited that I get to have this time with you" while also conveying the message "I have been around the block—and *you're* the one that really interests me." So, don't hold back, let the next person you like know it—it's an intimate and effective way to spark a new connection.[1]

7

The Seven Skills
of Deeper Dating

How to Lead with Your Gifts

Love takes off masks that we fear we cannot live without and
know we cannot live within.

—JAMES BALDWIN

In this chapter we'll explore how to lead with your gifts in your dating life, and how to let your gifts lead *you* in your search for love.
You'll learn seven Deeper Dating techniques that will help you
apply all that you have learned so far to your actual dating life.
These exercises will open new doors in your thinking, and change
your dating life in exciting and important ways.

HOW TO LEAD WITH YOUR GIFTS

Our Core Gifts lead us from the stagnancy of self-doubt into the
life-giving risks of authenticity. You've learned about how to honor
your Core Gifts and to access your Gift Zone. Now, what does it
mean to "lead" with the gifts you've been discovering?

Leading with your gifts doesn't mean you need to "put on" any
particular qualities—or to follow a fixed template of how to act.
How we authentically feel changes frequently. So what's the sign

that we are tapping into our gifts? A feeling of connection to our humanity. When we feel that sense of connection to our humanity, our authentic self comes alive We become more attuned to what we want and what we *don't* want. Finding that connection to our humanity, and then acting on it, feels risky but somehow exciting. It's an enlivened state that the Hindu teacher Paramahansa Yogananda called "balanced recklessness." In the world of dating, that might mean the following:

- Calling the person you're interested in

- Smiling at an attractive stranger on a bus—and if he or she smiles back, going up and saying hello

- Directly admitting to something you did wrong and apologizing

- Expressing a need or a depth of affection that makes you feel vulnerable or even embarrassed

- Telling your partner how you want to be touched during sex— or sharing an intimate sexual desire

- Saying "I love you" for the first time, not knowing how your partner will respond

- Entering into a new relationship, even after you've been badly hurt in the past

"Do I really want to put my soul on the line like this?" you may ask. "Is it worth the risk?" My answer is a resounding yes. When you decide to treasure and express your gifts, you gain the inner dignity and power that they bring, and your dating life—your whole life, in fact—will change. Your gifts will bring you face-to-face with countless risks, but they will be *your* risks, and they will widen and deepen you as you tackle them.

When we lead with an airbrushed version of ourselves we feel inadequate and insecure. Why? Because our false self *is* inadequate! It has no link to our personal power. It's like climbing a wobbly ladder. There's a constant feeling of uncertainty—and that's not what we want when we're dating. When we hide our true self, we find ways to sabotage real intimacy because we're scared of being "found out."

When our goal is to connect with our personal truth and to interact with the world from there, everything changes. We feel a sense of creativity and worth. Our fear of rejection becomes less tyrannical. Connecting with the world as we really are becomes our new passion. That is the art of deeper intimacy and it is dynamic, scary, and priceless. By practicing the following exercises you will learn important skills for evoking that state of intimacy, even in the earliest phases of dating.

A DEEPER DATING TOOL KIT

There's no way around it: dating is *hard*. Actually, the word *hard* doesn't begin to capture it. The disappointments, betrayals, blow-offs, and lies; the boring dates, the endless dates, the terrible dates; saying no to people who matter to you, being *told* no by someone you're interested in. The frustrations and dead ends—and yes, the wonderful, exciting, life-affirming moments, too—could fill volumes. Some people have simply given up on dating. Some, like you, haven't.

If you've completed even some of the main exercises in this course, you've touched the deepest and most precious parts of your being. How do you go on a new date, or meet someone online or through social media, and bring those parts of yourself into the process in a way that is appropriate for early dating? You've also worked hard to create safety and respect in your relationships. How can you enter the dating world—which is often *far* from safe and kind—and still protect your vulnerability? How do you lead with your gifts in ways that draw the right people to you? Let's look at seven skills of Deeper Dating that will help you bring your real self to the world of dating in a way that is much more likely to lead to real love.

These techniques require what may seem like a radical shift

from traditional ways of approaching the search for love. They all involve the deeper work of engaging your intuition, heart, and skills. Some techniques will come naturally to you. That's cause for celebration. Others will feel like areas you need to work on. With the support of your learning partner, you'll be taking real steps to develop and strengthen those skills. Some might seem too difficult to tackle. In those cases, refer back to "Loving the Lesson" (pages 125–26), which teaches a way to work with the parts of ourselves that aren't ready to change.

I encourage you to read all of the seven skills, and notice which one interests you most. And then pick only that one skill and work with it. Enjoy each new learning. The pleasure you take in your new skills will give them an even more solid foothold in your life.

1. Be Kind, Generous, and Thoughtful

Of the millions of words that have been written on how to win a mate, why do almost none of them tell us that kindness is one of the most powerful romantic intoxicants? In your dating life, don't be afraid to show your kindness. This advice might seem naive and risky, even inappropriate to the realities of a first date with a complete stranger. If you haven't cultivated the skill of discrimination, I might agree. But if you are committed to following only your attractions of inspiration, showing kindness and generosity is a very effective filter. When you are kind and thoughtful, you're being the person you want to be. Now see if your date shows the same qualities. If he or she cares about those traits and has worked on cultivating them, you'll know it almost immediately—and you'll have started things off in the best possible way. If your date doesn't show qualities of kindness, you'll find that out quickly enough, too! In either case, you'll get the information you need.

Most of us have been trained to be cool, not kind, when it comes to dating. "Next!" has become the modern dating call. If dating culture is anything, it's unkind. And amazingly, we have become used to it. With the multitudes of people many of us meet online and in dating events, we've lost the basic codes of kindness that create the possibility for intimacy. This has dead-ended countless potential relationships, and has led to a singles culture filled with deep loneliness. When romance and dating are separated from the simple truths of kindness and human decency, they begin to turn toxic, and without our awareness or consent, they steer us toward pain and away from love.

Yes, it's scary to show an extra degree of kindness and generosity. It exposes our soul. And that is exactly why we should do it! There is no better way than this to discover who is worthy of your core self. The next time you're on a first date, try showing just a bit more kindness and generosity from beginning to end, and then use discrimination to decide whom you want to date again based upon their response to your kindness. Kindness not only helps others; it leads us to meet kinder people, people who are capable of long-term healthy love. Kindness and generosity are intoxicating to others. They are the very medium of intimacy. Love is found, noticed, and cherished in tiny moments of thoughtfulness.

The writer Wendy Widom tells how one man's tiny act of kindness changed her future. At the time, Wendy was in her late twenties and living in Manhattan. She had convinced herself that her dream man would be much like Jon Stewart or a young Billy Crystal: a New Yorker with a slightly acerbic personality who enjoyed being the center of attention. So when she met a really nice guy from Cincinnati who was a bit shy and completely lacking in sarcasm—but who swiped his subway card for her—she was confused. She liked him, but he didn't match up to her picture of the man she felt she was destined to meet.

During their second date, it started raining, so she put her hoodie over her head. Her date reached out spontaneously and touched her head, really gently. She didn't expect that touch. She looked at him and realized that something had just shifted. She thought, *You're smart. AND you're nice. The guys I usually date are smart but don't always treat me so kindly.* He was outside the realm of what Wendy expected for herself. A year later they were married. In Wendy's words, "I would say I married the man of my dreams, but I don't think even my dreams were this good."[1]

If that small act of showing unfiltered affection hadn't occurred, this might have been their last encounter. His tenderness opened a portal, and they both said yes to it. The next time you feel tenderness, you might change your future simply by expressing it.

Many of us feel an awkward vulnerability when we express generosity. Expressing an extra degree of kindness might leave us feeling exposed. When we give something extra, we're vulnerable because we want it to be received with pleasure and appreciation. When we're with someone who can't do that for us, we begin to wonder if we've made a fool of ourselves. Our culture has eliminated so many opportunities for subtle acts of kindness as a result of the pace of our interactions and new technologies that allow less and less warm contact. Moreover, current dating advice tends to stress confidence and maintaining a carefully modulated distance to keep the other person guessing. Yet kindness, more than almost anything else, spawns healthy love.

MICRO-MEDITATION

The "Unlearning" of Unkindness | Two minutes

Where have you learned the lessons of unkindness—toward yourself and others—in your dating life? Can you think of a specific episode? How did that experience affect you? Take a moment to recognize how many direct and indirect messages you've gotten that told you it's not safe to be yourself in the world of dating. Acknowledge yourself for having waded through so much insensitivity—and for the fact that you are still committed to a better way.

Now try to think of someone you have dated who has shown an extra degree of kindness or generosity. Remember how that felt. Perhaps it even shifted your thinking. Simply take a moment to remember that person and silently thank him or her.

2. If You Like Him or Her, Let It Show

This may also seem like naive advice. You're supposed to play it cool, not show your hand and risk frightening off your date. Play hard to get. Don't act interested. In fact, research shows that letting someone know you like him is one of the strongest ways to turn a date into something more serious.[2] Equally important, showing your affection is an act of bravery—it takes real self-acceptance to show your affection, to rest your hand on hers, take his hand in the movies, or make a comment that hints or shows that you find him or her attractive. These acts of warmth may make the difference between a date that goes nowhere and one that leads to something special.

Of course, it's important to temper your displays of affection with an awareness that many people are cautious, perhaps even frightened, in early dating. If your gut tells you that your expression of affection is a spontaneous expression of your warmth, and if you sense that the other person might be ready, go for it. If it feels more like an inner plea or an outer ploy to get this person to like you, think twice before expressing it. You may well be feeling a sense of desperation because you're picking up on your date's essential unavailability. In other words, you may be sensing the first signs of an attraction of deprivation. Showing your interest shouldn't scare someone off. If it does, there's a good chance you're "going to the hardware store for milk." Keep using your sense of discrimination.

Janet had been dating Bill for a few weeks and she found that her feelings were really beginning to grow. Walking by a chocolate shop she saw a beautiful confection of dark chocolate and raspberries that looked luscious and celebratory. She fantasized about buying it for him and getting it gift wrapped, but then felt that such a gesture was too forward. She worried that it would make her appear needy. That it would scare him. She thought about it for a moment and realized with a start that he was different than the intimacy-phobic guys she was used to dating. He didn't seem like the kind of guy who would be scared by a box of chocolates (unlike the majority of guys she had dated in her life). She bought him the chocolates and walked to her date with an extra sense of happiness, her affection for him having grown just through her own generosity and the realization that he would not be frightened by it. And he wasn't. He was warmly delighted, and Janet had the dual experience of intimacy with him combined with a sense of inner freedom and personal growth.

3. Focus on the Quality of Your Connection

When we are on a date, it can be easy to devote too much attention to an inner scorecard we all use to decide whether the other person measures up to our standards. When we focus too much on that scorecard, we lose access to one of our greatest gifts: the ability to feel our connection with another person. According to the world-renowned psychologist and author Daniel Goleman, "We are wired to connect. Neuroscience has discovered that our brain's very design makes it *sociable,* inexorably drawn into an intimate brain-to-brain linkup whenever we engage with another person. That neural bridge lets us affect the brain—and so the body—of everyone we interact with, just as they do us. During these neural linkups, our brains engage in an emotional tango, a dance of feelings."[3]

By staying in touch with the feelings in your body and your heart, you can engage this linking-up process—and in so doing, learn so much more about the possibilities for emotional connection with the person in front of you. So, next time see if you can drop down past that exhausting "scoring" tendency and notice how you actually feel when you're with your date.

Jake and Paula met online and they eventually decided to meet for coffee. Jake was an artist, and Paula was a senior VP in a Fortune

500 company. Jake was a fierce Democrat, Paula was a staunch Republican. He was in sandals and shorts, she was in a power suit. She even stepped away to take a business call. It didn't look good.

Still, Jake hung in, and the conversation was pleasant, even enjoyable. But in his mind he knew this could never work. Her politics were unforgivable, and she seemed buttoned-down, almost rigid. Even so, when she walked away for her call, Jake tried the dating micro-meditation below to sense the quality of the connection. He checked in on his feelings—how he felt in his body, in his heart. And he was quite surprised at what he found. She made him laugh. He felt warm and comfortable, and challenged, but in a good way. He actually felt grateful that he had met her! If he hadn't taken those minutes to check in on his deeper sensing, he would have spent the time preparing a funny story about his ill-fated date. But this insight shifted his whole experience of things. Paula came back to the table, and she looked great to him. There was something he liked about her, and he wanted to see her again.

MICRO-MEDITATION

The Quality of Your Connection | One minute

This wonderful process will allow you to bring the intuition of your wisest self to any dating situation—or any interaction at all.

The next time you're on a date, see if you can get past the "mate or flee" response and into a gut-level sense of the quality of connection with your date. Take a break from the wearying stream of assessment: Does he like me? Do I like her? Instead, notice what you're actually feeling with the person. Of course you're probably feeling nervous. But in addition to that, do you feel pleasure? Do you feel warmth? Is there a sense of fun? Do you feel inspired? Unsafe? Criticized? Our minds tick off our checklist of what constitutes a catch while our hearts may be sensing something altogether different.

Rest with the feeling of your actual connection. This will help guide you to your next steps with the person you are with.

4. Practice Bravery

Bravery is one of the great skills of dating. For many of us, the biggest dating fear of all is of approaching someone new or asking for a date. It takes bravery to get out there and try to meet people.

Letting someone know you are interested in her is like building a muscle. You get better at it the more you practice. We often feel as though we weaken ourselves by letting someone know we like them. Another way to look at it, though, is that we're being generous. By showing our interest, we're giving the other person a compliment, and the sensitivity and decency of her reaction will tell us much about who she is.

I once took a trapeze workshop for complete beginners. I remember the scary feeling of climbing up tiny steps to a high, narrow platform. Of course I was tightly harnessed and roped in. If I fell I knew that I'd be gently lowered onto a trampoline-like net. Still, when I had to leap off that ledge into open space, it was pure, jet-black fear. The moments before leaping were very scary—but when I finally jumped, it was exhilarating. It's like that when you approach a stranger or let someone know you're interested. Each time you do it—no matter what the result—a part of you will feel stronger and more in control. And the more you practice, the easier it gets.

5. Discover the Art of Squinting

If you've ever watched an artist working on a portrait, you may have noticed that he pauses to squint. Squinting helps the artist capture the essence of his subject without getting distracted by its harsh outlines. We need to do the same in our dating life. It's so easy to get lost in the hard assessment of people's imperfections, and of our own. Often we hyperfocus on externals and miss the qualities that matter most. Squinting helps us get around this. I'm not suggesting that you force yourself to date someone you're not attracted to. But don't lose sight of the whole person because you're stuck on nagging external imperfections. Chances are, the person you will finally come to love will look different than the person you've fantasized about! Innumerable opportunities for real love have been lost because daters didn't know the wise skill of squinting.

Squinting is a technique to use in relation to a person's external attributes, not his or her important personality traits. For example, your date may have an unfortunate sense of style. Try to squint for now. Later, you can offer suggestions (which may or may not be followed!). Is your date nasty to the waiter? *Don't squint!* In fact, keep your eyes wide open. Sooner or later, the chances are great that she will do the same thing to you or your loved ones.

6. Share Things You're Passionate about and Ask the Same of Your Date

Keith Ferrazzi, the author of *Never Eat Alone: And Other Secrets to Success, One Relationship at a Time*, teaches about the importance of relationships in the business world and in life.[4] In one of his workshops I learned a very useful lesson. Ferrazzi asked us to break into groups of three and introduce ourselves to each other and chat for a few moments. The result? Discomfort, flat interactions, and polite, boring conversation. Next, he asked us to tell some details from our lives. That conversation was a bit more interesting—but not much. Then he asked us to share with the others something we were passionate about. I don't remember the details of what we discussed, but to this day I remember the actual sense of being a *team* that we all felt within five minutes. It was a game changer, and an eye-opener.

On your next date give this a try. Talk about what you are passionate about. Speak from your enthusiasm; the right person will love this. The wrong person may not. And that is very good to know. And then be sure to ask for the same from your partner. Notice what makes her glow and ask more about it. Doing this is giving her a gift, and most people will feel closer to you as a result. "What do you like to do in your free time?" might not be enough to evoke the response you want. People are trained *not* to reveal too much enthusiasm on an early date. If you're watching for signs of passion and not getting any, you could even ask him what kind of things matter most to him or give him the greatest joy. What, really, do you have to lose? Some people may feel too shy to answer a question like that, but if it turns them off to you, then you have the information you need right up front.

The following story tells about a woman who very successfully broke a few crusty dating rules in one fell swoop by sharing her passion. Danielle was a strong, fiercely intelligent woman with a wicked wit. Her feisty exterior coexisted with a very generous heart. She deeply wanted a relationship, children, and a family to love—the whole works. But guy after guy didn't seem ready for the challenge. She decided she was going to follow her dream and have a child—man or not. She began the process and joined a group of single women who had decided they were going to have kids. She decided to honor who she was and not wait for anyone to give her permission.

When she met Ryan, she waited for three dates before sharing this with him. They were on a hike together with a group of friends. She got Ryan aside and they climbed a rock together to enjoy the view. After a short while, she said, "Ryan, I like you, but I need to tell you who I am before I start getting my hopes up. I'm looking for a guy who wants to get married and have kids. That's what I want for my future—a family." It was terrifying to do this, but she had already preplanned this moment with her friends. She realized she was holding her breath as she waited, but she didn't have to wait long. He looked at her and said, "Where do I sign up?" Being Danielle, she smiled at him, picked up her canteen, and said, "That's great—I'm really glad. Now let's go catch up to the rest." Inside, she was celebrating. How long had she waited for this? And fifteen years later, these dear friends of mine are still together—with two great kids and a big golden Lab.

7. Become Fiercely Discriminating— About the Things That Matter Most

The dating world is challenging in so many ways. Yet you are now entering into it from a completely different perspective. You know your Core Gifts and you know their worth. You know about attractions of inspiration—and they are the only attractions you're looking for. If you're going to be brave enough to show your true self, then you must become fiercely discriminating about the people you choose to spend your time with. Is the person you're dating kind? Is he or she emotionally generous (even if quietly so)? Are you inspired by the way this person lives his or her life, and by the kindness and acceptance he or she shows you? If so, celebrate what you found and do your best to nourish it. It's a rare and precious thing.

But if you show your warmth, originality, power, vulnerability, or passion and he trounces on it, you have the information you need to make a decision. Or maybe you find that she is kind—and then coldly dismissive. Or thoughtful—and then almost nasty. If so, trust your gut. The key here is "eyes wide open." If you really want love that lasts, it's doubtful you'll find it there.

Deeper Dating Workbook

PERSONAL EXERCISE
Choosing Your Next Skill

Of the seven skills described, which one "chimed" for you? Briefly answer the following questions about it:

1. What made you choose this particular skill? Describe what struck you in thinking about your own dating life in relation to that skill.

2. Who feels like a role model for you in his or her use of the above skill? In which way is this so?

3. Picture yourself in the future, having grown in this skill. Picture who you will become as you learn to use it more fully and more bravely. Describe this "future you" in a few words or a few sentences. Take a moment to savor that picture of your future self.

LEARNING PARTNER EXERCISES

Planning to Practice Your Skill

Speak with your learning partner about the skill you've chosen and share whatever parts you wish from the "Choosing Your Next Skill" exercise above. Work with your learning partner to craft a concrete plan for a specific new behavior you are going to try on your next date—or in any relationship you choose. Support your learning partner in doing the same. When you both have decided on your plan, you will be ready to tackle your first Deeper Dating field trip. Following are the details for this field trip.

Deeper Dating Field Trip 1: Practicing Your New Skill

Now that you and your learning partner have made a plan to practice the new skill you've chosen, it's time to try it out in your life. Decide where and when you'll practice it (e.g., on a blind date I planned for Friday, or on my next date with Sarah). "Bookend" it with your partner; let each other know when you'll each be doing the field trip, and touch base afterward to share your reflections and "war stories." And don't forget to congratulate yourself! Admitting that an area needs work and tackling it in a kind and self-respecting way are hallmarks of a true "student of intimacy."

Optional Deeper Dating Field Trip 2: Bravery

This is an exciting and important field trip. If you can't do it with your learning partner, "bookend" it together. Let each other know when you are doing it, and connect afterward to share your experiences. Go somewhere and commit to approaching at least two people who are attractive to you and do not have the obvious characteristics of attractions of deprivation. See if you can make eye contact before walking up to them. If they don't notice you, go up to them anyway! Do it when you are completely sober. It's deliciously scary, and when it's over, you'll probably feel very proud. Your goal is not to get a single phone number or a single expression of returned interest. Your only goal is to strengthen your all-important muscle of bravery. As you practice this exercise, you'll find it becomes much easier to smile at someone on the subway platform, to ask someone if she is enjoying a book she has in her hands, or simply to say hi. Go with your learning partner or a friend and do it together. Connect throughout the night to catch each other up and share war stories, and afterward, go and celebrate. If you don't feel ready for this exercise, modify it to something easier, such as asking a friend to introduce you to a person you are interested in.

If you attempted this exercise, congratulations! You've earned a new badge of dating bravery.

8

A Deeper Dating Guide to Finding Love

*Where to Look—And What to Do
When You Get There*

If you want to end your isolation, you must be honest about
what you want at a core level and decide to go after it.

—MARTHA BECK

Now that you are learning how to lead with your gifts and build
attraction in a healthy relationship, let's take this show on the road.
It's time to explore where to look for love—and what to do when you
get there.

Let's be real: the dating world can be a really cold place. Most
venues designed for meeting single people are shallow at best.
Winking, texting, and one-sentence profiles just don't encourage
deep communication. Dating events rarely leave us feeling great
about ourselves. And most inspiring cultural events aren't designed
with single participants in mind. Yet there are great tools available to
every single person. In this chapter you'll learn to use these meeting
tools, but you'll add an essential ingredient: your authentic self.
When we take back (or *occupy*, if you will) our authenticity in the
cynical land of dating, we dramatically improve our chances of finding a real soul mate.

I spent my twenties immersed in many dimensions of the singles world, not realizing how lonely I was, how empty I felt, and how many potential opportunities for building a rich life passed me by because of my passionate involvement in the club scene and my never-ending attempts to find love. I went out night after night looking for love, and went home night after night, sometimes alone, sometimes with someone. But I was playing out the same patterns again and again. Search for love, seek validation for my looks and my worth through people's response to me, find sex, and realize in the morning that this certainly wasn't going to be love. It's really easy to do that, especially when you're young.

Some lucky younger people know how bankrupt the bar and club scene is and don't have a compelling interest in it. But many do, and it takes years before they realize the emptiness they have been living in. I started realizing this when I began therapy after years in the singles scene. In those years I had become compulsive in my search for love and sex. And as I began to open up to the softer parts of me, parts that I had tried to suppress for so many years, I began to feel a yawning loneliness so huge that I could find no words for it—a loneliness that I had never let myself feel because I was too fixated on the next conquest and the next opportunity to meet "the one." And that fixation stopped me from feeling how sad and rigid I was becoming. This may not have been your experience at all, but it is pretty clear that the dating scene hasn't been much of a warm bubble bath for any of us.

When I lead Deeper Dating events, I can often see the great discomfort that participants feel just at being there. I can see that they carry with them the disappointment, the frustration, the history of endless insults to their humanity that they've encountered in their search for love. The process of finding love comes with real risks, but so much of the pain of dating comes from the way we treat each other.

For older people, and perhaps most especially for older women, there can be a sense of fear as the clock ticks. At one Deeper Dating event an honest woman in her late fifties put it simply: "I'm scared. I'm getting older. It's a buyer's market for men in New York. I don't want to get old alone. And I don't see much hope." As we get older we find that we've aged out of the dating websites and dating events. Many clients have said to me that once they hit their forties the number of responses to their online profiles dropped significantly. And once they hit their fifties, sixties, and onward that number plummeted even more.

The machinery of the singles scene chews us up in our twenties and thirties and spits us out when we hit our forties, leaving many of us feeling battered and lonely. As long as we are getting recognition in singles events, clubs, bars, and websites, we remain at risk of being sucked up in the stampede that may seem like the only available way to find love.

But here's the heart of the matter: whether we're in our twenties or in our nineties, we must find a way to disengage from the toxic, degrading, and dehumanizing approach toward love that we're taught, and learn to engage in a wiser, kinder, and more self-honoring path.

I won't deny that for many people it's indeed harder to date: for a seventy-five-year-old woman living in a small town, a sixty-five-year-old man in a wheelchair. Yet I have seen many people in these situations and others find lasting love by shifting their approach to the one I describe in this book. No matter what your age or life circumstances, there are wonderful people out there looking for someone like you. After years of experience in this field, I am virtually certain of this reality.

Let's explore some of the many options currently available for finding a relationship: real-life venues, dating events, and online dating sites and apps. Try these approaches out. I think you'll see your dating life change in concrete ways that bring you hope and a new sense of possibility.

LOOKING FOR LOVE THROUGH YOUR CONNECTIONS

Start with the goodwill of the network of connections you've already developed and earned. This is an example of cheating at the maze. Start right at the center—with the people who know and appreciate your gifts. It is likely that the people you know have devoted many years to building their own circle of relationships of inspiration. The network of cultivated healthy connections you can tap into is vast—and there's no reason not to save time and energy by engaging it. This is known as working smart instead of working hard. Many of us don't reach out to our friends and family to let them know we're open to meeting anyone they think is a good match for us. Or if we do it once, we don't remind our loved ones to keep their eyes open for us. Save yourself time and start here. Jamie Cat Callan, the author of *French Women Don't Sleep Alone: Pleasurable Secrets to Finding Love*, shared this with me:

> French women don't date, at least not in the American fashion, interview-style date. Rather, the French (and most Europeans) meet at dinner parties. These parties can be formal or very casual, potluck style. They're often intergenerational and include family and friends and new acquaintances. A dinner party is a great way to get to know someone in the context of friends and family. It buys you a lot of time, because you can be just a friend for quite a while before it becomes something more serious. Also, there's no exchange of money for an expensive dinner, so there's no pressure. And even after meeting up at dinner parties or going out in groups, the French still do not date but rather they'll go for a walk together. This gives both parties more time to get to know one another before deciding to become romantic. So, basically, it's about becoming friends first and getting to know one another in the context of friends, family, and community before jumping into bed.[1]

See if you can find creative ways to use your network of caring friends and family to help you in your search. For countless generations, that's how many people have found their mate. Here are some suggestions.

1. Ask a number of close friends and family if they know someone they think might be a match for you. Be sure to ask if anyone comes immediately to mind for them. If they seem enthusiastic but come up with a blank at first, you might even ask them to look through their social media connections. Check in with them for their responses the next time you speak—and occasionally thereafter. You can even do this via e-mail. Ask your friends in a way that's not perfunctory but from the heart.

2. You have friendships of inspiration. Go to these friends' parties and events. Ask in advance if there will be anyone you should keep an eye out for, and if so, ask them to introduce you.

3. Be creative. Use technology. New apps appear regularly that allow your friends to tap into their pool of contacts to introduce you to new people. Take advantage of that opportunity.

4. Your single friends know lots of single people. Form a shared approach, a kind of dating-pool co-op. Think of all the people you don't wish to date who might be a match for a friend of yours. Take the time and effort to help make that connection—and ask the same of them.

5. Many of your dates won't work, but that's okay. You've already created a superior filter; give yourself the space to simply meet these people and give them a chance.

LOOKING FOR LOVE WHEREVER YOU ARE

Love can happen anywhere, and when you are in your Gift Zone, the possibilities for new connections increase. In that zone, you *notice* more things, such as someone's lovely smile or a beautiful detail on a building that you've never really noticed before. Your Gift Zone is imbued with a kind of magic. Expect the unexpected when you dwell in it and follow its prompts.

John Salvato, a Deeper Dating teacher, told me that at a Deeper Dating event someone asked, "Where do you meet people?" Someone else volunteered, "On the street." From the back of the room another participant eagerly asked, "*Which street?*" On some level it doesn't matter where you are. When you're in your Gift Zone, anywhere you happen to be could be the place to find real love. In the streaming flow of this zone, connections can happen at the supermarket, on the street, or anywhere you may be. Life will unfold in a different and richer way if you're feeling connected to your gifts. When we're feeling brave, and connected to the warmth of our humanity, our chances of meeting someone special increase exponentially.

The author and blogger Sarah Bridge offered a creative alternative to the singles dating scene in her blog post "Do Single Events Make You Feel More Single?" She wrote, "I am learning to make every minute a potential door to a date. I sit at the front of the bus and make eye contact with people rather than heading straight to the back. . . . I take different routes, visit different places, get out of my routine. I walk with my head up, with open body language and smile or even chat to complete strangers in the coffee shop, at the supermarket, on the lift at work. People have been astonishingly receptive: it seems everyone is looking for an 'in,' a reason to say 'hi.' . . . It's nervewracking but fun and an ego-boost when a smile or overture is returned. Now that I've started looking around, it seems that everyday life is full of friendly single guys, while dating life—well, not so much."[2]

1. Follow Sarah Bridge's example in your day-to-day life. Try new routes, go to new places, make eye contact, and be open to new people you encounter.

2. The next time you're out walking, shopping, or running errands, try a Gift Zone experiment. First, do your activity in the normal way. If you're like most of us, your mind will be on your to-do list or any number of possible subjects that have little to do with the present moment. Notice what that's like.

Now take the next part of your walk in a different way. Find a way to move more into your feelings, your Gift Zone. Walk at a pace that allows you to feel more human and less like an accomplishment machine. Notice what that's like, and how different the world feels. Notice people as you do this. Enjoy seeing dogs, people with kind faces—anything inspiring. And if you want to steepen the dating-adventure gradient, smile at anyone who looks attractive to you. Afterward, you might even want to take a few moments and write some notes on the contrast between your experiences trying each of these two approaches.

NONDATING EVENTS, GROUPS, AND GATHERINGS

Going to events filled with strangers is awkward and challenging. It's so much easier to surf the Web in your sweats and comfy T-shirt. But if you really want a good relationship, take my advice: get out of the house—and don't make a bar your first choice. When you're looking for the person who will become "home" for you, start by looking in the best places: venues that spawn comfortable, values-based interactions. In what venues would it be most likely that your Core Gifts will be welcomed, invited, and received with appreciation?

After being single for many years, my friend Mike is now in a great relationship. He recently told me what he did to find love. He finally accepted that he had to go to gatherings with people who shared his passions. He said to me, "Ken, I'd come home from work and just want to turn on the TV and relax at home. It sometimes almost made me sick to go out to meet strangers again and again, but I knew I had to. And that's how I found my partner Steve."

You want a partner who knows how to give. Someone who cares about things that matter. Someone who shares at least some of your Core Gifts. These people are your path to happiness. They are the ones to seek out. The best place to meet them is at the events where they naturally congregate: service organizations, religious or spiritual groups, gatherings of people who share your passion for the outdoors, for art, or any other interests. I know it's hard to dive in and do this, but it's a wise and effective way to look for love. Many of us follow the herd by leaving our *romantic* self out of values-based events, and leaving our *deeper* self out of dating events. Try doing the opposite! You have a right to approach people and even flirt at nondating events, if you do so in appropriate, nonintrusive ways. And you don't have to cover up your depth at a dating event—even though almost everyone else may be doing just that.

Begin with a local listing of events and find those that speak to your passions and interests. What have you been dying to explore but haven't found the time for? Meditation? Dance? Photography? Now is the time! Use your network of friends and connections to generate new ideas and find out about new events, and plan to attend them.

See if you can go to an event at least every two weeks. You'll find not only that you are meeting more potential dates who share your values but that your life is also enriched. Is this hard to do? Absolutely! That's why you need a learning partner or friends to support you.

When I was wrestling with the decision to adopt a child, I worried that having a child would stop me from finding a partner, that free time would become a thing of the past, and that I'd simply never be able to retire because of the astronomical costs of child rearing. My mother reminded me of a German saying: "Each child brings its own luck." She suggested that my luck would actually be expanded by having a child. This has turned out to be so true. My son actually led me to my partner. The joy of my bond with my son led me to create Deeper Dating, to write my blogs and this book, and to develop Gift Theory. "Each child brings its own luck" has many different meanings. For example, every action where you assert your uniqueness, express your passions, and follow your dreams is like a child that you're creating, and your brave act sends ripples out into the world. More often than we might imagine, those ripples find their way back to us. Don't minimize the power and the possibility of doing things that you love and that excite you—even if they seem unrelated to your search for a relationship.

1. Notice your patterns at events like this. Do you interact with others? What types of people do you interact with? Do you put your desire to meet someone on hold, saving that for dating events?

2. Remember to look for inspiration, and to respond to it, whether it comes from a ninety-year-old or a child. Inspiration leads to inspiration! Inspiring people know other inspiring people, and some of them will be single and searching. Don't reach out only to people you are attracted to. Try to build connections with anyone who inspires you by their presence, even if it's only for friendship.

3. If you use a geosocial app for meeting, this is the place to turn it on. It will help you connect to others, and find single people with shared values right at the event.

4. If there is an ongoing community of people with shared interests, such as a social, political, or religious group, consider becoming a part of its social fabric.

5. When you're there, try not to just stand alone. Find a way to talk to people. Try to engage, interact, and ask questions.

6. If you grow to make friends in that community, let them know that you'd like to be introduced to people they think may be a match.

DATING EVENTS

Dating events can be a wonderful tool for meeting lots of people, but they can also be really hard. Many opposite-sex events have unequal numbers of men and women. Many leave you feeling defeated if you don't find any matches. Be careful about which events you choose; some are better than others. Seek out events that attract people with deeper values. Try a variety of them and see which work best for you.

At these events it's easy to feel insecure. And when we feel unsafe, we are more likely to revert back to old, unhelpful patterns of interaction—or avoidance of interaction. Here as anywhere else, keep your eye for inspiration wide open. If someone isn't exactly your type but attracts you in some way and inspires you with his warmth, creativity, or decency, be sure to get his number. You may at least find a new friend.

Practice kindness at these events, including to those you're not attracted to. And practice being kind to yourself. When you don't get a match, you are confronted with what is probably the biggest obstacle to deeper intimacy in your life: self-criticism. The temptation to feel less-than or unattractive is very compelling. It is also toxic, unhealthy, and illusory. Until we can get past these crushing feelings, we will not be able to take the risks inherent in dating, and in loving. This is an opportunity to build a skill set that will help you avoid feeling crushed by the common experience of "getting no matches."

1. Notice which people you choose. Don't just choose people with whom there is an intense physical attraction. Be open to attractions of inspiration where the spark may be less intense. Attractions can grow!

2. Were there others you wanted to approach or choose but didn't? What stopped you? What could help you to do it next time?

3. Were there any behavior patterns that you'd like to change or refine? Speak with your learning partner or someone else about this and make a plan for trying a new behavior the next time you attend an event like this.

4. Acknowledge yourself for any behaviors and attitudes during the event that felt healthy, brave, or self-accepting.

5. Be willing to come back and try again. Maybe you and your learning partner could attend an event together and you could try out your new refinements together.

6. Often after an event we only follow up with the people we were strongly attracted to. In cases where there was only a mild attraction, we frequently drop the ball. Even in the case of a mild attraction, something in that person made you note him or her as a match. Do follow up.

ONLINE AND MOBILE VENUES

The proliferation of online dating tools allows us access to a breathtaking range of possibilities for meeting people. If you're looking for love, don't ignore these tools, but use them in new and creative ways without getting lost in the dehumanizing numbers-game mentality they can create. With the skills you've learned, you can combine the power of the Internet with the effectiveness of real intimacy skills to speed your search for love.

Dating Websites

There are countless dating websites. Most of us assume that the only viable dating sites are the monoliths we all know about. There are countless smaller "niche" dating sites that focus on a wide array of interests, hobbies, and activities. Whatever your passions, there's a good chance there's a dating site for people like you. Also look for websites that offer events, meet-ups, and offline activities. Explore some of the countless online communities of interest where, over time, you can get to interact with people who share your passions and interests. If there is a particular type of person you are looking for, you may find websites that are specially designed to help you meet that type of person.

The sheer number of possibilities on dating sites has a numbing effect on us, making it all too easy to shut down to the humanity of each new contact. With all the choices we have, we tend go for the safest bet—the people we're most physically attracted to. Don't get seduced by numbers or be limited by the requirement of instant intense sexual attraction.

If you meet someone *reasonably* attractive, who seems like a potential attraction of inspiration, resist the temptation to move on and look for someone more attractive. If someone seems worthwhile, be sure to follow through. By practicing the techniques in chapter 7, you'll be developing new skills on almost every date, even the ones that don't lead anywhere.

When you write your profile, share your authentic self. Don't worry too much about being witty; try to be real. Showing that you took the time to write a thoughtful, spell-checked profile will make a big difference in weeding out the wrong people—and studies show that more thoughtful profiles get more responses. (However, don't write a profile that's extremely long.) Describe your passions. Show your heart. Show your profile to your learning partner or a friend to see if it conveys a sense of your Core Gifts. I encourage you to share your real age. For those who just don't feel comfortable marking the correct age range in their profile, Julie Spira, the founder of CyberDatingExpert.com, has a smart solution; she suggests posting some great pictures and then sharing your real age somewhere in the body of the profile.

When you surf through profiles, take the time to sense what's between the lines. Look for signs of inspiration. When you find those signs, reach out if it seems there might be a potential spark. You're in this to win this. Stretch your age and location parameters a bit. Allow yourself to be *surprised* by the shape love takes. Start with a wider field, and narrow it down based upon the individual.

The same basic rule applies no matter how you date: lead with your authentic self. Use the apps and the websites, but don't hide behind them; quickly get real and show your authentic self.

1. Within the limited structures of a particular site or app, try to find a way to show your real self. Some meeting apps allow

you only a few words to describe yourself. In that space, be real! Your goal is *not* to meet as many people as possible. With the stratospheric number of people you can meet on-line, your dance card of random suitors can take up all your days and nights. Your goal is to limit the field by attracting the real thing. Don't worry about all the people who'll be turned off by your (appropriate) authenticity. You don't want those people anyway.

2. As quickly as possible, come out from behind the screen of charming but empty anonymity provided by these sites and apps. Show your authenticity. Show your kindness. Make it clear early on that your intention is not to chat forever, but to speak on the phone and then to meet.

3. Have more than one picture. Spira suggests that you invest the time to look for pictures in which you shine, pictures from times when you were full of life and enthusiasm. Look for pictures that show your face reflecting the glow you feel when you experience a real connection to your gifts. Let the pictures capture you in the most flattering way, but make sure they are recent, not oversexualized, and that they capture the way you really look.

4. Remain kind and gracious. Other kind and gracious people will notice and appreciate it—and those who don't are the ones you *don't* want to meet. On your date, listen, ask questions, and show interest. And if you like the person, let them know. Remember that research shows that sharing your vulnerability and your interest in the other person (in appropriate measures) are two of the keys for creating attraction.

5. Don't just respond to the hottest candidates with the sexiest pictures.

6. Follow through with all appropriate connections you make. Speak on the phone before deciding whether you are interested.

This person may have special qualities that you won't discover unless you speak—like a really sexy voice or a great sense of humor. If someone is even somewhat attractive and it seems like she may be an attraction of inspiration, try not to drop the ball simply because there are so many more intensely sexy people online. That's a hall of mirrors you don't want to get lost in.

BARS, CLUBS, AND SOCIAL EVENTS

Most people will at some point—perhaps lots of points—find themselves in bars, and all of us attend a variety of social events. Bars are set up to trigger what I call LCD, or "least common denominator" connections. Don't drink too much. When we do that, we lose the extra resilience, insight, and heart that help us practice new behaviors. If you meet someone who is drinking a lot, be aware that the person you see drinking will probably be a different person when sober.

1. Notice the specifics of your patterns. What do you tend to do in a bar, club, or social event? Do you approach people? Are you shy or outgoing? What kinds of people are you most likely to approach? How do you approach them?

2. Once you've noticed your patterns, try some new ones. Try approaching—or sticking with—people who seem like they might be attractions of inspiration. Watch out for traces of nastiness, intense superficiality, and slickness—and stay away.

3. Take the risk of speaking to people if you can. See if you can make it into an adventure. Notice who smiles at you. Perhaps smile back at these people.

4. Take the time to notice who is interested in you. We often have no idea when people are looking at us. If you're with a friend, support each other by pointing out who seems interested in him—and vice versa.

5. If you are seriously looking for a relationship, my advice is to try to stay away from quick hookups. If you are at a bar or club, and there's someone who interests you and has any sense of real potential, leave and go somewhere else where you can get to know each other more. If not, try to find a quieter section of the bar to get to know each other. Exchange numbers and make a date. Again, if this is someone you feel could be a potential match, you will gain a lot by not having immediate sex. This is not about morals or ethics. I know some people who have met the love of their lives through a hookup! God knows, I tried to do just that for many years. However, when our level of sexual intimacy doesn't match our actual closeness, the tendency for one or both partners to flee increases dramatically.

SETTING AN INTENTION

Many people have a tendency to define dating success by one criterion: Did I meet someone who could become *the one*? Now that you're approaching your search for love as an intimacy journey, you can also create new definitions of success for yourself. Setting an intention is an exercise created by the Deeper Dating instructor (and one of my main dating mentors) Hernán Poza. This exercise can change any dating experience into a journey of growth and adventure.

Setting an intention changes the way you feel before, during, and after an event. Try this exercise when you're searching online, walking down the street, in a bar, or at a party. There are countless possibilities for intentions. Choose one that interests you most at the moment. Here are some examples:

- I'll approach two people I'm interested in. Whether they're interested or not, I'll consider the event a success if I take that step.

- If someone isn't interested, I'll move on. Period. I won't keep trying to get them interested in me, and I won't lose hope and leave. If I can do that, I'll be doing something really different.

- No matter what, I will be kind to myself and other people. Even if I don't meet anyone, I'll be proud if I can simply act thoughtfully toward everyone.

- If someone seems like an attraction of deprivation, I won't waste time with him or her as I have often done in the past.

- I won't just hang out with friends at this event. I'll take ten minutes and stand alone so people will have the chance to approach me.

Try setting an intention in any environment where you think it might be possible to meet someone. Done regularly, it will help you reclaim a sense of power, control, and sanity in the often dehumanizing world of dating. Going to an event with a friend and supporting each other in following through with your intentions will make this process all the more enjoyable.

Deeper Dating Workbook

DEEPER DATING EXERCISES
Choose One Activity

Choose one activity and suggestion from this chapter that "chimed" for you and that you feel ready to tackle. Just one. Share it with your learning partner, and then make it happen. Try not to ignore the first three categories; they may be the hardest ones to do, but if you're really serious about finding love, they may well be your best bet.

Online Your *Way*

Brainstorm with your learning partner and come up with three interesting and creative new ways that each of you can harness the power of the Internet in ways that suit you. Each of you should choose one of these, try it out, and report back to your learning partner.

LEARNING PARTNER EXERCISE
Practice an Intention

In addition to sharing your experiences with the exercises just described, decide on an intention before an event or before going online, and share it with your learning partner. After you try it, call, text, or e-mail your partner with a brief postmortem.

9

Taming the Great Saboteurs of New Love

Though you consciously long for a mate, there are parts of you that do not, that push the idea away, that hasten to lock the door when the other part of you has so carefully opened it.

—PAT RODEGAST AND JUDITH STANTON,
Emmanuel's Book: A Manual for Living Comfortably in the Cosmos

Whether you're single or coupled, it's natural that parts of you will want to flee the very love you're hoping to build. A common belief is that fear of intimacy is a pathology, a condition that makes one unsuited for lasting love. In the old binary model, either we have "intimacy issues" or we're essentially just fine. A deeper and more useful understanding is that all of us have fear of intimacy; what we do with that fear is a marker of who we choose to become in the world. Fear of intimacy is a basic condition of being human. It's not a "flaw" any more than fear of dying is a flaw. If we're breathing, we can assume we have fear of intimacy.

In fact, admitting the ways we flee love is an act of personal courage that adds firepower to our search for love. When we admit the "flight patterns" we've created to avoid the deep risk of love, we have the chance to break those patterns and adopt new ones that serve us better. *We do not have to rid ourselves of our fear of intimacy before we can find healthy lasting love!*

In this chapter you will learn about the single most powerful destroyer of healthy relationships, which I call the Wave. You'll also learn one simple, powerful, and gentle question you can ask yourself at any time, which will bring you right to the heart of your ways of fleeing love. Act upon what you discover, and your dating life will open up. You have my guarantee.

THE WAVE OF DISTANCING

In my years as a psychotherapist, dater, friend, and learning partner, I've come to believe that one phenomenon has destroyed more potentially great relationships than any other single factor. I call this phenomenon the Wave of Distancing (or simply, the Wave). The Wave occurs when we push a caring and available person away by inwardly diminishing his or her worth. Our lack of training in the phenomenon of the Wave has led to the loss of countless relationships. Groucho Marx captured this experience perfectly when he quipped, "I don't care to belong to any club that will have me as a member."

What does this phenomenon look like in dating? You're dating someone caring and available, and there has been at least a spark of attraction for you. And yet:

- You can't find the sense of affection and desire you once had.

- You keep getting irritated at him or bored by him.

- Her flaws make you quickly lose respect for her, even if you don't show it.

- You start yearning for the excitement of the hunt.

- You feel like a fraud, pretending you're still interested when inside you just don't feel it anymore.

The Wave manifests itself differently for different people. Some people experience it as boredom. Some become extremely judgmental about the person they're dating. Others might fixate on how much they dislike the other person's laugh, or on a physical attribute they find unappealing. Some just find that their interest has evaporated for no good reason at all.

In the past, when I would find someone special and then realize he really was available and interested, the Wave would hit me in predictable ways. I would feel a sick sensation inside, a dread mixed with a suffocating sense of obligation. I'd feel guilty and disappointed in myself, but I'd feel certain that my interest had fled and would not come back. There was only one viable option—escape. And that is precisely what I would do. I lost decades of my dating life to the Wave. More than any other factor, it was the Wave that kept me from love.

This widespread phenomenon has huge implications for our romantic lives. If we can't navigate the Wave, we'll keep going after the wrong people and passing the right ones by. Our lack of training in managing the Wave has doomed countless good relationships. In many of the workshops I have led throughout the years, I have asked for a show of hands from those people who felt their romantic life had been affected by the Wave, and in almost every case, the majority of participants instantly raised their hands. Conversely, many people have saved a wonderful relationship just by recognizing the Wave for what it is—a temporary distancing of our partner that springs from our very human fear of intimacy—and responding to it in a new way.

Have you ever gotten close to a bird's nest that had eggs or baby birds in it? It's a very disconcerting experience. The mother bird's most precious possession is in danger, and she does extreme things to keep you away from the nest. She may attack you, or she may act as if she has a broken wing, distracting you from getting closer to the nest. These actions are desperate instinctual responses to having her nest endangered. When we meet someone who is available and decent, something inside us knows this person can get to our "nest," our soul, the place where we care the most and can be hurt the most. And our unconscious panics. It does whatever it can do to frighten the person away. Like the protective bird, it creates a ruse, anything at all to keep the nest safe. And the Wave is one of the most powerful ruses our psyche can find. If we think that our attraction to someone has disappeared (or we forget that it was ever there), our first thought will be to flee.

What do you do when the Wave hits? The great secret to the Wave is found in its name: it really is only a wave—and waves pass. When I tried to quit smoking, I was also struck by the wave-like quality of my urges. When the urge came, it didn't feel like a want—it felt like a *truth*. Down to my bones, that cigarette felt *necessary*. Amazingly, though, once that hypnotic and compelling wave of desire passed (and it always did), I would come out the other end deeply relieved that I hadn't lit up. When you hit the Wave in your dating life, try not to panic and try not to flee. *It will pass.* In most cases, your affection just went temporarily underground and will reemerge if you handle the Wave skillfully. Even though you can't feel your affection at the moment, it's most probably still there. Give yourself a bit of space—you're allowed to do that!—and keep a sense of goodwill toward the person you're dating. It can help a lot to speak with friends who can remind us of what we like about that person. Sometimes a simple, "Are you nuts? This guy is great!" can be enough to bring us back to our senses. And when the Wave passes, you'll probably find an added benefit: you'll have a clearer view of who this person is and what you feel for him.

Danny had been dating Jill pretty seriously for about a year but found himself doubting the relationship. Was this the right person? Was she "the one"?

He was in a café with his good friend Tom and he told him about his doubts. "Should I continue with Jill?" he wondered.

"You've told me in the past that you loved her, even though you're not feeling it at the moment, right?"

"Yes . . . "

"Do you think she loves you?"

"I know she does."

His friend, normally quiet and understated in manner, looked him in the eye and said, in a voice that was a quiet yell, "Danny, are you out of your fucking mind?" Danny was embarrassed, but in the end he was very grateful. Something shifted inside. He remembered how attractive Jill was, how funny and how nice she was, and he thought, *Tom is right*. When he saw Jill a few hours later, the love and appreciation was back. He needed that jolt to be brought back to the reality of how much he valued her. Danny realized in that moment that on some level, love and attraction are really about making a choice. We can kill a great relationship just through our doubt—or we can use our efforts to help it grow.

Here are six keys to handling the Wave:

1. Try not to allow worry or fear take you too far off course. In the great majority of cases, the Wave passes, even though it can be very disturbing when it hits. Don't assume your feelings have truly disappeared. That will make you even more anxious and even more prone to flee.

2. Take the space you need in a gentle way. Don't make a big deal of it. Don't overreact by picking a fight, criticizing the other person inordinately, or doing things to alienate or upset her.

3. Do. Not. Pressure. Yourself. You are in a process of getting to know the other person—and in fact she may not be a match for you in the long run. Don't pressure yourself into having sex before you're ready, or into seeing her more frequently, or moving to a monogamous relationship more quickly than you're ready to do. Any time we feel pressured and pushed by guilt or obligation, we may well experience the Wave as a result. Remember: You have every right to follow the pacing that works for you. Don't flee, but take the space you need in order to continue the connection.

4. Try to find the gratitude, the pleasure, the sexual turn-on, or the fun you've felt before with this person. Do the things you enjoy. Touch and hold and have sex if you wish—in the ways you love most. Try to connect with your Gift Zone when you're with him. The Wave is largely a manifestation of fear, and positive, safe connection relieves fear.

5. Discuss your fear with your learning partner, a friend, or a therapist or coach. Take the time to explore and work with that fear.

6. If there's a conflict or a sense of discomfort with the person, try to work it out. If we suppress our gifts or feelings, we will be much more prone to the Wave. If this is the case, it may be better to speak to that person and see if you both can work it through. In many cases you'll find the Wave simply lifts and disintegrates the moment the problem is raised and worked through.

You may experience the Wave at different points in a relationship and in different ways. Some people are happily married for years, and then, when it's time to consider having a child, the Wave hits with a giant crash. Sometimes people experience the Wave in the beginning of a relationship and never experience it again. Mark, the physical therapist whose story is told in chapter 4, moved in and out of the Wave for years with Sarah, and after he asked her to marry him, it never came back. It's up to you to understand and to learn how the Wave manifests for you, what triggers it, and how to move through it and come out the other end.

Paradoxically, experiencing the Wave may be a clear sign that you are in a relationship with great potential. Usually we only feel the Wave with people who are available, so if you're experiencing it, it means you've grown to the point where you're focusing on someone who isn't running away. In fact when you are in the Wave it may be time to celebrate! The Wave is more likely to occur in attractions of inspiration. As a psychotherapist I often *wait* for my clients to experience the Wave. They won't experience it as long as they are chasing attractions of deprivation.

I'm not advocating that you settle for less, or that you discount your intuition when someone doesn't feel right for you. What I am suggesting is that you let the Wave pass, and let the affection wash back in. And then see how you feel. Do that as many times as you need to. It may change your dating life.

Some of us feel the Wave more strongly than others. The degree to which you're ashamed of your Core Gifts is usually the degree of intensity to which you will feel the Wave. The more shame or trauma you feel around your Core Gifts, the more you will be at the mercy of the Wave. But none of that means you can't find love. It just means that the whitewater sections of your Wave are going to be stronger and possibly more frequent.

Some of us are more prone to the Wave because of past traumas. When we risked our heart in the past and were met with coldness, distance, or abuse, we came to believe that there was something shameful in our vulnerability. So now, when someone becomes vulnerable with us, our old wounds come back and unconsciously instruct us that there is something shameful in our *partner's* vulnerability. The more we've been shamed for our vulnerability, the more we will be susceptible to the Wave. It can be tremendously helpful to do deeper therapeutic work to heal these wounds. But the techniques I'm describing can still help immensely when the Wave hits, whether or not you choose to do additional therapeutic work on the underlying issues.

Sometimes it's not the Wave; it's just that the other person is actually not right for you. You cannot force yourself to be physically attracted to someone. If your lack of attraction continues, you are not obligated to stay with this person. It's not good for you and it's not good for her. But if you find that your attraction waxes and wanes, be sure to read chapter 11 before making any final decisions. It might open up new possibilities for you.

MICRO-MEDITATION

The Wave | Three minutes

Have you ever been hit by the Wave? Remember back to a time when you pushed away someone decent and caring because her availability frightened you. Take a moment to thank her for her good qualities. If you wish, you can internally apologize to her, letting her know that you were doing the best you could without an understanding of what was happening. The great news is that now you can name this phenomenon, and you have a set of steps to follow when it hits. Try to forgive yourself for being a victim of the Wave. Know that you are one of a vast number of people who have never been trained to understand and handle this phenomenon. Appreciate yourself for what you've learned and for the ways this new understanding will change the outcome of your future search for love.

DISCOVERING YOUR "FLIGHT PATTERNS"

The Wave is not the only way we flee love. Because we're human, we care, and in every place we care we can be hurt. Love is the place where we care the most. The more we love, the more that love can be taken from us. Therefore, all of us protect ourselves in some way or another from the fiery heat of pure love. We do it in myriad ways—and we need to forgive ourselves for the fact that love scares us.

It's so easy to criticize ourselves in our search for love. There's always something we could have done better. We can't correct all the ways we flee intimacy—it would take until the end of time. However, if you can find one prime way in which you push love away—and if you tackle that defensive pattern, you will see the love in your life increase and deepen. That choice is a small act of personal greatness—and it is within your reach. If you want to do something that's going to make a huge difference in your search for love, address this pattern. It will create a new opening in your life.

One Way You Flee Love

The following exercise will help you name one way that you flee love—even as you seek it. Give yourself time to read this small but powerful parable, and then take a bit of quiet time with your journal, and follow the simple instructions that follow it.

> A woman was intently searching through her yard. A passing friend asked what she was looking for. She told him she had lost a pair of extremely valuable earrings, which she had last seen in her living room. Her friend asked the obvious question: "Well, why aren't you looking there?" The woman answered, "It's so dark inside. It's much easier to search out here."

In this story, the "living room" is a metaphor for the place where you know the real work lies but which you'd prefer to avoid. In your search for love, what is your own "living room"? Here are a few possibilities—there are many others as well. Trust your gut response to this question.

- Do you waste time trying to make things work with the wrong people? Remember, if you are dating someone whose values do not inspire you, you're ultimately wasting your time.

- Do you show your "soul"—that is, your passions, your tenderness, and your quirkiness, to people who inspire you? Do you share your emotional and sexual edges? (In the appropriate time frames, of course!) Or do you show an airbrushed, less original version of yourself?

- Are you taking the time to meet people who share your values, in real-time, nonvirtual settings?

- Is there important inner work that you need to do, such as addressing emotional, sexual, or addiction issues that hold you back?

- Are you so busy looking for a relationship that you're shutting out the intimacy that already exists in your life with family, friends, or pets? When we become so desperate for love that we ignore the love we already have, we frequently sabotage our own efforts.

- Or are you simply too busy? When we're too busy we miss the moments that might lead us to connect, or to feel our feelings, or to move into the richness of our Gift Zone. In our Gift Zone, we are more likely to remember a friend who lives far away, or to smile at a stranger sitting right across from us.

This is an important moment in your journey. With your journal in front of you, take a moment to reflect on your own patterns. What is your "living room"? What is the pattern that stands out as the most important way that you are avoiding intimacy—even as you seek it? Write down your most honest answer to this question. When you've answered it, take a pause to congratulate yourself. Most people never get this far. *The act of facing this will change you.* Address this issue, and your search for love will change in big and important ways. It's that simple.

WHAT TO DO WITH OUR FEAR

Now that you see how you may be fleeing love, you are probably wondering what to do about it. Remember, lasting change almost never comes through pulling yourself up by your own bootstraps. We heal through relationships. It is through respectful, caring, pleasurable connections with friends, family, social groups, and professional helpers that we free ourselves from the loops of smallness and the knots of behavior patterns that keep us from the love that we seek.

All of us have a fear of intimacy, and all of us need to find ways to address that fear in our lives. As we struggle to find a way to handle our fears of intimacy, the story of Lil and Joe may hold some valuable insights.

Joe Lucca was a teenager on vacation in Rehoboth Beach, Delaware, when he had an accident that would change his life. He was bodysurfing with friends when a powerful wave grabbed him, flung him wildly, and crashed him headfirst onto the sand, snapping his neck. His friends carried him out of the water, and he was rushed to the hospital. When he came to, Joe discovered that he was permanently paralyzed from the neck down. A few days before, he had been a carefree teenager, not even questioning the reality of a full life ahead of him. Now all he could imagine was indescribable emptiness. He sank into a terrible depression. His girlfriend gradually stopped visiting him, and then broke it off. Joe spent years in hospitals and rehabilitation facilities. In time, he came out of his depression and began to build a life for himself. He even dated a few girls and began to look for work.

Lil was a nurse in a nearby town. One day a friend asked her if she would be brave enough to go on a double date with two paraplegic guys. Lil was up for the adventure and said, "Sure." Her date was an aggressive and obnoxious guy, but the other guy—Joe—was quiet, kind, and respectful, so when he asked her out, Lil said yes. They had a great time, and their dates became a weekly event. Lil told me, "I liked being with him because he was gentle, kind, never aggressive, and very interesting to be with. We discussed anything and everything. That's how the relationship grew—first friendship, then love." During that time, Joe was able to find a well-paying professional job, and after three years, even though he was terrified to do it, he proposed to Lil. And she said yes.

What allowed Lil and Joe to get over their hurdles of fear and trepidation? Recently I asked them that very question. Their answer was transcendent in its simplicity.

"We just kept spending time together because we wanted to. We didn't think of marriage at first. That would have been way too scary. We just let the closeness build. At a certain point, we realized that our love and respect for one another had somehow become bigger than our fear. After that, it was just a matter of putting one foot in front of the other." Lil and Joe are in their eighties now, and still very happy together. Lil told me, "I feel that I would be lost without Joe. It's a tenderness. It's laughing together, living together, and doing the things that bring *life* into our lives."

What's Joe's advice for anyone who is afraid to risk stepping out and looking for love? "At some point you have to take the leap. The alternative is loneliness. Hey—if *I* did it, so can you."

Not all of us have the courage of the Luccas. And that's fine. Remember, we do not have to rid ourselves of fear before we can find healthy lasting love! We must jump in and learn the ins and the outs of our personal minefields. The wisest path is to accept our fear instead of seeing it as an aberration. When we learn to stay present for love in the face of our personal fears, our lives open up. As Joe and Lil's story shows, the greatest antidote to fear of intimacy is intimacy itself!

Deeper Dating Workbook

PERSONAL EXERCISE
The Wave

1. When you read about the Wave, did you feel it related to you? When have you experienced the Wave in your relationship history? What did it feel like? And what happened as a result?

2. What might you do differently when the Wave hits, now or in the future?

DEEPER DATING EXERCISES
Ask Your Loved Ones

This exercise is strong medicine—but it works. Ask your friends to tell you how they have seen you flee intimacy even as you seek it.

Often our close friends wish that we might do something differently in our search for love, but they are hesitant to tell us. Ask them if they have any advice for you concerning what they would like to see you do differently.

Pick One

Choose one way of fleeing intimacy to tackle first. Only one. You will be working on this with your learning partner this week and in the future. If you don't have a learning partner, see if you can find other supports to help you make this change.

LEARNING PARTNER EXERCISE
Changing One "Flight Pattern"

Share the pattern that each of you has chosen to address. Go into detail about how this pattern manifests, and how it affects your intimacy life and your search for love. Be very careful not to offer advice unless your learning partner asks for it. Make a plan to address your flight pattern. Chart out the steps—including other sources of support. And continue checking in around your progress. Don't assume that one conversation on this topic will be enough.

10

How to Find the Light in the *Middle* of the Tunnel

The very least you can do in your life is figure out what you hope for. And the most you can do is live inside that hope. Not admire it from a distance but live right in it, under its roof.
—BARBARA KINGSOLVER, *Animal Dreams*

The middle phase of the journey is one of the hardest parts of the search for love. You have the sense of new possibility that comes with choosing a gift-based path to love—and you've seen changes already—but you're still out there, navigating through the dating world, and you haven't met your beloved. This is a period where you might feel bewilderment and confusion, where love doesn't seem to be coming quickly enough. In this phase it's good to see and appreciate how far you've come, and to consider how to bring the genius of your gifts into the journey ahead.

STARTING IN THE RIGHT PLACE

When the road becomes hard and the weather rough, the place to return to is always the same: acknowledgment of what you already have and of how far you've come. If you have been following the ideas in this book with a sense of care and focus, it is almost certain that you have already experienced changes. Try answering the following five questions to reflect upon your progress on this journey.

1. Do you understand and value your gifts more deeply?

2. Are you losing your taste for your attractions of deprivation, and getting away from them more quickly?

3. Are you increasingly following your attractions of inspiration?

4. Are you expressing your authentic self more in your relationships?

5. Are you taking steps to meet new people?

Every question you answered affirmatively is cause for celebration. If you answered yes to at least two of the above questions, the chances are great that your dating life is changing in significant ways. It is very possible that, almost mysteriously, you're meeting kinder and more available people. Trust the path you're creating—because it's working.

If, however, you honestly feel that no significant changes are occurring for you as a result of this work, ask yourself the following five questions. Usually at least one of them will hold the key to explaining the stuck point you're experiencing.

1. Are you in an actively abusive relationship of any sort?

2. Do you have any untreated emotional or psychological disorders or an active addiction?

3. Are you doing this course on your own, without a learning partner or support?

4. Are you resisting putting your heart into these steps?

5. Is there another issue, such as an old relationship that you haven't been able to let go of, that is blocking your progress?

If you answered yes to any of the above questions, this may clearly explain why your progress is being blocked. I encourage you to take the brave step of getting appropriate help and support for yourself. Then all of the positive changes you are making will have a chance to take hold in a more solid way.

MICRO-MEDITATION

How Far You've Come | Three minutes

In our intimacy journey, every lesson we learn moves us closer to the love we seek. Of the lessons you've learned since you began this course, which one feels most important to you? It doesn't have to be big or grand, but it should be a change that truly matters to you.

Take a moment to reflect. When you have your answer, find the words—your words—that capture it best. Then take an important moment with yourself: hold your accomplishment close to your heart and appreciate it. (Yes, your learning was imperfect. Yes, it was limited in some ways. But it is perfect enough to move you more quickly to the love and intimacy you're seeking. So, it fully deserves this moment of appreciation.) Afterward, rest for another moment. Feel the ripples that may come. This savoring is a powerful way to deepen your learning.

This difficult middle phase of the journey is filled with less obvious manifestations of growth. If you are following these steps, change *is* happening—even if it's hard to recognize. In this phase you may feel as though you're stuck at the same old familiar crossroads you've confronted before in your dating life. It may feel as though nothing is different. But things *are* different. If you look more closely you will recognize that you are coming to these familiar crossroads with new tools, a stronger sense of connection to your own gifts, and hopefully with more support. At each crossroad you'll find yourself making new micro-shifts in your approach, and those shifts will open up new doors. You'll sense that something new is happening because you'll feel intimacy at a point that once felt like a closed door.

There are skills to be gained in this stage that can't be gained anywhere else. Just about every challenge you face and address in wiser ways will make you more skilled in your next relationship. And the more intimacy skills that you learn at this stage of your dating life, the more likely that you will choose a future relationship that can bring you long-term happiness.

I've found that it's rare that we move from no relationships, or unhealthy relationships, right into "the" relationship. There are still periods of being single that last longer than we would wish, and false-start relationships that frustrate us no end. I've found that it's usually more like a stepping-stone process. If we have been prone to unhealthy relationships in the past, there is often a process of encountering healthier-but-not-healthy-enough relationships, and leaving them more quickly than we would have in the past. Identifying these relationships—and learning to say no to them—is one of the skills many of us learn in this middle phase of dating.

THREE STAGES TO AN INTIMACY-RICH DATING LIFE

I've found that three stages forecast the advent of real and healthy love. Love's arrival might feel like a stroke of luck. But it's much more than that; you've been *inviting* that luck by approaching your dating life differently. Notice which of these three stages apply most to you.

In Stage 1 we learn how to embrace our gifts and honor them. There is a sense of healing in this stage as we learn to honor our tenderness, our intuition, our power, and our core spirit. With that comes a deep distaste for anything that *dishonors* these qualities in us. At a certain point—and usually as a result of tremendous pain—we begin to lose our taste for relationships that chip away at our sense of self-worth. We find we just can't stomach the thought of being hurt like that again. And this is a great thing. When we become less "sticky" to these kinds of attractions, a dead-end era of our dating lives is finally coming to an end. Now we can begin the real work of intimacy—cultivating our attraction to relationships that feed and nurture us. In dating and in all our relationships we start to clean house, emptying our lives of any unnecessary interactions with relationships of deprivation.

While you do this bear in mind that in most cases—barring the presence of abuse—it's best to give every relationship a chance for healing. If we don't tell our loved one what hurts and what we need, we may be depriving them of the opportunity to change. Relationships are precious things and worth the effort and work of healing. Don't just walk away! Give the relationship a chance to change for the better. This doesn't mean you will tolerate bad behavior; just that you're willing to see if it can stop.

Stage 2 holds a different challenge. When we let go of negative relationships, new friendships, better ones, don't come rushing in. In fact Stage 2 is often marked by a bewildering quietness. This stage may feel boring, discouraging, or frustrating. It seems as though nothing is happening. However, this period (which often seems to last far too long!) is an essential part of the process of change. Something is happening—we just can't see it yet. As with a bulb that needs a period of dormancy to gather its forces, deep changes are happening that haven't yet manifested in new bonds. Why does this part of the journey go so slowly? I believe it's because the change is so deep that it takes time for our full self to catch up.

In cases where we have ended abusive or painful relationships, we need time to heal. In the early part of this stage, there is often a need for alone time or some form of support in our healing. As this stage progresses, we start itching for new life and new love, and when it doesn't come as quickly as we anticipated, it's easy to feel discouraged. It helps to remember that Stage 2 is a part of the process, and to keep your eyes open for early signs of Stage 3.

In Stage 3, an amazing phenomenon begins to occur. As we begin to honor and express our gifts in our dating life and in other relationships, our world begins to change. New, healthy relationships gradually enter our lives. This stage usually starts with glacial slowness, as a new generation of relationships springs up in small new shoots. Often this happens so subtly that we don't even notice its occurrence. We find a new friend who inspires us. Or perhaps our calendar now shows some new events with people we respect and admire—and with whom we feel emotionally safe. In this stage, we gradually find ourselves dating people who accept us for who we are, people who are kind, generous of spirit, and available. Perhaps our sex life begins to touch new levels of intimacy and experimentation. Old and dissatisfying friendships become less a part of our day-to-day lives, and richer relationships begin to move to center stage. I often need to point out the beginning of this stage to my clients. It happens so gradually that they don't even notice it. It is likely that these changes will begin in your friendship life and then find their way into your dating life. In time we find that our relationship life has become richer and more vibrant, yet at the same time more emotionally safe. This is worth celebrating.

Please remember that these stages are not ironclad. We may occupy a few stages at once, or go back and forth between stages. This process of relationship growth may occur in our romantic life, our family life, or our friendships—or in all of these areas at once.

As we begin to fill our lives with healthier connections, we need to develop new skills of intimacy that allow these relationships to flourish. The following exercise teaches a gift-based approach to communication that has the power to change your relationship with yourself and those you love. The more you learn and practice this technique in the middle stage of your journey, the happier and more fulfilled you will feel, and the more successful you will be in all your close relationships.

THE AHA PROCESS—A SIMPLE TOOL
FOR BUILDING INTIMACY

The AHA technique is a three-step process that allows you to interact with the world from the heart of your Gift Zone. AHA is an acronym that stands for authenticity, honoring, and action. Each step is an act of empowerment. Together these steps create a gentle, skillful "overthrow" of the inner voices that hold you back. You can use this simple process anytime you want to connect with the power of your Gift Zone. The example I use involves a relationship conflict, but you can use this technique with any feeling or experience at all.

Authenticity

The initial step of this process is authenticity. The task of this first step is to connect with your inner experience right now. If you can sense whatever you are feeling and hold it with a quality of warmth and caring, then you have already moved into your Gift Zone. Settle into that experience, and it will lead you somewhere good and worthy, even if the feelings you have are challenging. When we are in our Gift Zone, healing happens naturally.

If you are not yet in that state of compassionate authenticity, well, join the crowd! It often takes some work to get there. First, give yourself a chance to settle in. Relax a bit and notice what you're feeling in your body. Imagine moving toward the center of your target and notice what's going on. Sometimes you won't be able to locate a feeling. Sometimes hunger, fatigue, or stress will get in the way. But at other times you will sense something, even if it's like a subtle scent in the air that you only occasionally perceive. You won't always get to a feeling, but the more you do this exercise, the easier it will be to find your emotions. If you can sense any feeling at all, find a few words that capture it for you. It may take a while for the words to form. Give yourself that time. Or perhaps there won't be words, just images, memories, a passage of music; all of these are fine. Allow your psyche to surprise you with what emerges, even if it doesn't make sense yet. Once you find such an expression, you have already created a degree of compassion for yourself, simply by that act. (If you find this step continually difficult, or if you'd just like to learn more about sensing your feelings, I highly recommend Eugene Gendlin's seminal book, *Focusing.*)

This initial settling-in phase can be uncomfortable. As you relax, the awkward or uncomfortable feelings you were able to ignore in day-to-day life may rise to the surface. Whatever we don't want to face may make itself known at this time. Therefore, when you do this first step of the AHA process, you can expect that there may be a bit of inner resistance—a kind of "speed bump" that tries to get you away from the challenge ahead. You might think, *No, I don't want to do this now. It's too uncomfortable.* Or, *I don't have time.* Or, *It's too much work.* These feelings are frequently the first guard at the gate to the treasure of your Core Gifts. Every time you walk past that guard and continue on to a felt sense of your humanity, it's an act of small courage; it's a step toward a richer connection to your Core Gifts. Sometimes when we check in with our inner state, our first thought is *I'm not feeling anything.* To grab the tail of your feelings a bit more, you can ask creative questions, such as "If my inner state were a color, what would it be? If it were a piece of music, what might it sound like?" Sometimes there will still be nothing. In those cases don't pressure yourself. Over time, this process becomes easier to do.

Here is how this first step played out for my client Jennifer. One of Jennifer's Core Gifts is a strong sense of loyalty and responsibility. When she's close to someone, she is loyal, even when it hurts. This quality goes hand in hand with her sense of responsibility. She rarely changes a lunch date, even if she's busy. If she says she'll be somewhere, she'll find a way to get there, come hell or high water. Tell her something confidential, and you can be sure it will stay that way. When she doesn't get the same back in return, it hurts and angers her. In her past Jennifer had many painful experiences with people who lacked her fierce sense of commitment. Because she was not able to name this attribute as a Core Gift, she constantly alternated between self-blame and the certainty that the world was composed of jerks—mostly of the male variety—who let you down when the going got tough. She hadn't dated anyone for three years when she met Douglas. She felt an essential sense of trust with him, and that was a new experience for her in her dating life. Unfortunately, Douglas was a lot looser on the issue of punctuality than she was. He would change their dates in a way that seemed almost cavalier to her, often delaying them by an hour or more. Occasionally he would break a date on the same day if his boss asked him to stay late. Usually Jennifer suppressed her anger when that happened. She would tell herself that she was being too sensitive. At other times, though, she'd fume and get critical, sometimes even nasty. Finally, she decided to acknowledge her feelings. She realized that she was furious at Douglas, and that made her feel very guilty. She felt torn in the same way that she had felt countless times before. As she allowed herself to feel these feelings, she realized that underneath her anger was hurt. She didn't like feeling vulnerable in this way, but it made her realize something: Douglas was starting to matter to her in a deeper way.

Honoring

The second step is honoring. This is the step that most of us are likely to miss, because we haven't been trained how to do it. Yet without the act of honoring, it's almost impossible to obtain the leverage we need to heal the patterns that hold us back from finding love. The honoring of our inner experience—no matter what it is—is the step that changes everything. It is impossible to find your Core Gifts without honoring your feelings—because that is exactly where your Core Gifts lie! This step frees us from having to suppress our true feelings or act them out.

How can we learn to honor our authentic experience? By noticing what we feel (step 1) and then finding the worth in it—*before* we try to repair it, change it, or improve it. Our feeling may not be perfectly on target. It is rightfully said that "feelings are not facts," but within our feeling, whatever it is, there is an inner truth trying to make itself known. Until that inner truth is validated, we usually remain stuck. Following are two questions you can ask yourself to help validate your experience. Try each one on until you feel an inner "YES!" When you feel that, take time to feel the ripples of relief that may come up for you.

1. It makes *sense* that I feel this way because . . .

2. This feeling touches a treasured part of my being because . . .

When we are feeling something we think we shouldn't feel, our first step is usually a reflexive act of self-correction, which can leave us cringing against our own self-critique. Answering these two questions is a conscious act we can do to honor our experience. Honoring the worth of our emotions—no matter what they are or how little we or others understand them—is a skill that changes the entire tenor of our lives. The table below will help you recognize the thoughts that signal that you are *not* honoring your experience. The next time you feel or think any of the thoughts in column 1, try replacing them with the corresponding thought in column 2 and try answering that question. I think you'll be delighted by the clarity they bring. When you honor your authentic experience, you will discover the deep gift that lies in its heart. And that gift will lead you to new freedom and new love.

Self-doubt	*Self-honoring*
What's wrong with me for feeling this way?	In what way does this feeling make sense?
What will people think of me?	What do *I* think of this? How is this feeling an authentic message from my inner self?
How can I fix this part of me?	What does this part of me *need* now? What's the worth and the value in that need?

Self-doubt	Self-honoring
I need to toughen up.	What if my strength came from honoring my vulnerability and then making choices to take care of myself?
I feel humiliated and ashamed by my feeling—and that makes me too uncomfortable to reveal my authentic self.	What is the Core Gift within this feeling?

When you seek to understand what you're authentically feeling and to honor it, the answer may not come right away. Don't worry about that. Just stay open, and in time it will make itself known to you. Remember, these are not gimmicks. These are deep and profound practices of self-love and intimacy. The answers often won't come right away. These periods of not knowing are part of the true adventure of intimacy.

In the long run it is the act of honoring that is the antidote to our bewilderment and the path to our own unique genius. The act of self-treasuring may be challenging, but ultimately it's the most comforting path of all. Every other path hurts. Everything else is broken glass, sharp brambles in our side. Honoring is the skill that enables us to live the beauty and mission of our Core Gifts in the world. Honoring requires giving up the whip we wield against ourselves; it requires a kindness, a listening to our gifts. Our gifts are at once too powerful, too original, and too tender to be ordered around by us. They will *never* stop drawing outside the lines. And if we try to make them do so, they will hide in plain sight until the threat is gone. No matter how much we threaten or pressure them, our gifts won't come out until they sense they will be honored. It's that simple. *Anything less than honoring is essentially an act of violence against ourselves*. We cannot dishonor our Core Gifts without repercussions.

Sometimes there has been so much feeling around a gift that we need to rest with it—to not go any further quite yet. Simply holding it with a sense of care is enough.

> I hold my face in my two hands.
> No, I am not crying.
> I hold my face in my two hands
> to keep the loneliness warm—
> two hands protecting,
> two hands nourishing,
> two hands preventing
> my soul from leaving me
> in anger.
>
> —THICH NHAT HANH

Honoring also includes the honoring of our external reality. For example, is this person someone who has earned the gift of your authenticity? Does she seem like someone capable of honoring your vulnerability? (Have you honored hers?) If so, that's a wonderful thing. If not, you might want to be careful in what you share with her.

By the way, honoring isn't only for pain. It is for positive emotions as well. For example, it is often an act of bravery to share tenderness and appreciation, or simply to take the time to relish your joys. Every time you feel joy or peace, you've reached a pleasure portal to your deep gifts. This is what you've worked for and hoped for. When you feel a moment of tenderness, treasure it. When you feel joy, take pleasure in it. Let it guide you. As it has been said, what you appreciate, appreciates.

It is also an act of intimacy to honor the reality of the other person's gifts and wounds. Who is the person you are interacting with? How might her own sensitivities be involved in this situation? Allow yourself to honor her humanity as well. Take the time to put yourself in her shoes.

When Jennifer got a promotion, Douglas told her he'd like to take her out for a special celebration dinner. She was very touched.

No one had ever done that for her before. Two hours before dinner, she got a call from Douglas asking if they could delay their meeting time by an hour. Jennifer was very hurt—and absolutely livid. She also felt guilty for the intensity of her reaction. She noticed that she was swinging between fury at Douglas and judgment of herself for being so angry. This time she decided to practice honoring her experience. First, she talked to herself in a different way: She tried to see how her feelings made sense. Here's what she came up with: "It makes sense that I feel this way because I wouldn't have done the same with Douglas. I would have done whatever I could to keep our date, and if I couldn't, I would have felt badly and let him know. I felt vulnerable because he was taking me out to celebrate my promotion tonight. No one has ever offered to do that before. All that got ruined when he delayed the date so easily.

"I take my commitments seriously. I am aware of what it means to be someone who keeps her word. This is one of the qualities I treasure most about myself. When it comes to loyalty, this is who I am: I give a lot, and I ask a lot, too. I am different from most people in terms of how much this matters to me, but that's who I am. It's connected to my deepest values. Whomever I'm with will need to honor that in an essential way."

Now she let herself think about Douglas and who he really was. In reality he had never let her down in big ways. Yet she didn't know what he would be like if she really let herself rely on him as a partner. She was uncertain—and that was fine. They had only been dating for a while, and it was a valid concern. As she thought about it more, she realized that he often did special things for her. He was, in fact, more generous than she was, and more consistently kind. As she realized this, she had a short bout of self-doubt, and began to feel slightly guilty about harassing him. She thought about not saying anything. Why was she so demanding anyway? But finally, she decided to try practicing this technique. She would honor him, but she'd honor herself too.

With that decision, Jennifer began to relax inside. The anxiety she had been feeling came from her uncertainty about whether or not this quality of hers was *acceptable*. When she decided to honor it as a Core Gift, the war inside was over. Self-doubt had been replaced with self-honoring.

Action

The final letter of AHA stands for action. In this stage you hold your inner self, and that of the other person, with honor and act on that in whatever way feels wise, true, and helpful. This step can be so hard. It takes biting the bullet. It takes time after time of doing it clumsily and gradually becoming more skilled at it. Finally, it is a leap. In the words of Maggie Kuhn, founder of the elder rights activist group the Gray Panthers, "Speak your mind even if your voice shakes."

In the excitement and vulnerability of authentic action, your ability to find love is increased. When you take the action of honoring yourself and the other person, and you're met with the same, your heart will open. It's an amazing feeling.

Douglas could tell how angry Jennifer was, and he called her back to say that he was able to push the time back; they would only need to delay dinner by 30 minutes. Jennifer was still angry, but that made her feel a bit better. She planned to wait until after dinner, but Douglas brought it up almost right away, apologizing again. Jennifer felt mollified but decided to still tell him how this experience affected her.

She began by expressing what she appreciated about him, including his offer to celebrate her promotion. She revealed that she had a lot to learn from his natural and free-flowing generosity. But she also told him how she felt hurt about what happened. How hard she tried to keep her appointments and how let down she felt when other people didn't do the same. Douglas got a little defensive, explaining that his boss really pressured him to stay. She told him that this didn't make her feel better. His offer of a celebration dinner made her feel vulnerable — and he let her down. She acknowledged that this was a sensitive spot for her, and she told him why. Then, she said something that was really hard for her: she was starting to care about him in a deeper way—and that's why this hit her so hard. Then Douglas was really able to hear her. He told her that he felt the same way about her. He said that he was really excited about the possibility of a future together and he felt very bad to have hurt her. Those were just the things she had wanted to hear! Jennifer was used to men putting her down when she tried to share her difficult feelings about something that was happening in the relationship. She had been internally braced for being shamed for her vulnerability, but Douglas did the very opposite, and she appreciated that greatly. As a whole, they both felt very good about each other after the conversation. Jennifer felt openhearted in a new way, and even closer to Douglas than before their conflict. Equally important, her endless inner war between self-doubt and bubbling resentment was for the moment laid to rest, simply by choosing to honor herself and Douglas in a new way.

Through action our authentic self is formed in the world, and that action lets us begin to have the influence upon the world that we were born to have. Then we can finally give our Core Gifts the responsibility and respect they need to grow up and find their maturity. That is when we can feel both vulnerable and worthy at the same time. Without the capacity to honor yourself and take wise action, your unconscious mind will protect you from real love because it knows you can't take its heat. It protects you because it knows that you would either do damage to others with your anger or do damage to yourself by caving in to their needs and demands. When you know how to honor yourself, your unconscious will open the padlock protecting your gifts because it finally trusts you. Every time you practice this process, the part of you that can love is strengthened. The more you do this process, the richer your life will become.

Jennifer found a way past her old coping style, which pushed love away. In fact, by honoring her own gifts and her boyfriend's, she brought them closer than they had ever been. We have a great power to deepen the passion and love in any of our relationships simply by modulating how much we let ourselves "go in" toward the center of the target.

MICRO-MEDITATION

Your Next Brave Step | Three minutes

When we are in the middle phase of our search for love, it is often hard to know what new steps to take. Close your eyes for a minute and think about the millions of "shoulds" around dating that might be spinning in your head. "I should go out more. I should redo my online profile. I should lose ten pounds."

Now let those go. Simply let them go. You're looking for a Guiding Insight here, not a "should." I want you to go closer to the inner rings of the target—your Gift Zone, where your heart speaks. And ask yourself: What might be my next brave step? Take a minute and see what arises for you.

It doesn't matter what it is. It might be that you attend a workshop, or start exercising regularly. It just matters that it comes from your heart, and it feels true. See what comes up for you.

Now take a moment to notice what feelings come up as you imagine taking this step. See if you can commit to it. Acknowledge yourself for both your honesty and your sense of adventure.

Deeper Dating Workbook

PERSONAL EXERCISE
Your Core Gifts Handbook

Your Core Gifts are part of the "central nervous system" of your entire intimacy life. In this important exercise, you will come to understand the inner workings of one essential Core Gift. Choose one Core Gift that you would like to understand more fully. It may be the Core Gift you discovered in your tears (pages 53–55), the Core Gift discovered in your joys (pages 40–44), the Core Gift your Gift Circle revealed to you (pages 75–77), or the Core Gift you feel timid about revealing (page 65). You will have answered some of these questions before; others will be new. As you answer each of the ten questions below, you will come to understand your relationship life in a new way. With that understanding, you will have an invaluable "user's guide" for this Core Gift, spanning your romantic, sexual, spiritual, and emotional dimensions.

A copy of this Core Gifts Handbook exercise is also found in the appendix on page 243. You can also download it as a pdf from the Deeper Dating website (page 241). You can repeat these same questions with any Core Gift you'd like to understand in a deeper way, and put them together to make a Core Gifts Handbook, which will be a user's manual for dating and for your whole life.

1. Describe your Core Gift in one sentence.

2. What image, piece of music or art, or personal memory captures the essence of this gift when it feels most accepted and alive?

3. Name one person in your life who consistently understood, valued, and appreciated this gift. Describe how you feel when your gift is honored in this way.

4. In what types of situations does this gift feel most deprived of oxygen? Describe the pain you feel when this occurs.

5. Describe the ways in which you suppress this gift in your relationships.

6. Describe the way you act out defensively around this gift in your relationships.

7. Describe your deprivational "type": someone who attracts you but can't really honor this particular gift.

8. Describe the kind of person who makes you feel that this gift is valued and appreciated.

9. How would your romantic life change if you shared this gift more fully—with the right people?

10. How might this Core Gift be a pathway to a richer, fuller life for you?

This exercise is also your learning partner exercise. If possible, go out and do this field trip at the same time and in the same place as your learning partner, and then go out afterward to share your experiences. If that's not possible, speak about this field trip when you've completed it, and if you want extra encouragement, speak to your learning partner before you go as well.

Judgments

At one point when I was feeling particularly sick of all my dating failures, I went to Harold Kooden, a clinical psychologist and a gifted expert in issues of intimacy for gay men. He gave me the following exercise. I will never forget how shocking it was—and how helpful. Try this one wherever there are potential dates. It's pretty strong medicine, but it will change the way you view things.

You can do this anywhere. Simply participate in whatever activities are occurring, but notice every judgment you have about others—and about yourself. Be honest with yourself about what you're thinking. After fifteen minutes, stop, find a private space, and list every judgment you had. Share what you noticed with your learning partner. You'll probably be shocked by what you wrote, but that's good. The shock of recording our judgments is sometimes enough to disable them immediately. The next time you think these thoughts, you may recognize what you're really doing—pushing people away and putting yourself down. In an atmosphere of judgment and criticism, intimacy dies and isolation flourishes.

Cultivate Lasting Love

In Stage 4 of the Deeper Dating journey you'll learn how to build sexual passion, romantic love, and emotional depth in the new, healthy relationship you'll find—and how to build deeper intimacy into your life as a whole. Passion and intimacy grow in very different ways in healthy relationships than in unhealthy ones. You'll learn how to grow these qualities in a safe and stable love. You'll also discover one or more of your most important sexual and romantic Core Gifts. Finally, you'll discover how all the lessons you've worked on weave together to form a foundation of happiness for your upcoming romantic relationship, and *all* your relationships—including your relationship to yourself.

The Old Map to Love

You must act confident to attract a great partner.

The New Map to Love

Authentic self-confidence, mixed with sensitivity toward others, is profoundly attractive. But that kind of confidence is built when we *accept* our vulnerability and needs and stop trying so hard to transcend these essential parts of ourselves. When we suppress our healthy needs, they fight back by turning into neediness.

Our needs and our vulnerabilities are inextricably woven with our Core Gifts. If we try to amputate them, our psyche will fight for its life with all the wiles it's got. I am not suggesting that you need to share all your insecurities with someone you're starting to date, but I am saying that the vision of coolness, wit, and charm that we are taught to portray is impossible to attain. Brené Brown, a researcher who studies vulnerability, shame, and human intimacy, captures how most of us feel about vulnerability: "It's the first thing I look for in you, and the last thing I'm going to show you."[1] Brown's research shows that sharing vulnerability—which means sharing our innermost self—is the key to the kind of love that can last and grow.[2] It's endlessly seductive to think we can transcend our vulnerabilities and radiate confidence to attract love, but that myth can make us lose years of our life seeking an invulnerability that we can never attain—and which would in fact render us incapable of the love we're seeking.

11

Cultivating Sexual and Romantic Attraction to People Who Are Good for You

Your Sexual Core Gifts

For the first time in his life he understood why the Bible called sex "knowing."

—DAMON SUEDE, *Hot Head*

We can't force our attractions. Most of us have learned that the hard way. However, we can *educate* our attractions, and that can change our entire romantic future. When we learn the skills for cultivating sexual and romantic passion in our healthy attractions, we can start building the kind of love we wish for. When we learn how to educate our attractions, our dating life opens up in a new way.

In an attraction of inspiration, a spark of attraction has the potential to grow into a flame if we know how to nurture it. Even if you're relentlessly attracted to bad-boy or bad-girl types, or to unavailable people, you can still develop this capacity. These are the same skills you will use to keep passion alive in your future relationship. They are lifelong skills of romantic and sexual intimacy. By using these skills in a healthy relationship, you can blend intense sexual turn-on with the joy of intimate love. And really, what is more wonderful than that?

THE ATTRACTION SPECTRUM

All of us are attracted to a certain type that stops us dead in our tracks: a physical type, an emotional type, and a personality type. Let's say that there is a spectrum of attraction, from 1 to 10, and the people at the low end of the spectrum (numbers 1 and 2) aren't physically or romantically attractive to us at all, but those on the 10 end of the spectrum are compellingly attractive, they make us weak in the knees, and they trigger both our insecurities and our longing.

How does the spectrum work? Every time we enter a room of people, we make choices based upon our attractions: Whom do we notice? Whom do we pass over? Often, these don't even *feel* like choices. Some people simply attract us, and others don't. Yet there are deeper forces at work, many of them below the radar of our conscious awareness. Deb, a young stockbroker from Chicago, once told me, "You know, it's almost magical. I can go to a party, and there's always one person I'm most attracted to. If I date him, within a few weeks or a few months I discover he has the same emotional qualities as my previous boyfriend. But when I first saw him from across the room, I had no idea at all that this would be true!"

When we encounter someone for the first time, our eyes, our psyche, and our heart begin an astonishingly complex scan, noticing obvious physical characteristics such as age, gender, height, and weight, but also picking up subtle cues such as body language, facial expression, the contour of the lips, the nuance of the voice, and the muscles around the eyes. We instantly process all this information without even knowing it. All we feel is desire or the lack of it. Scientists tell us that the silkworm can sense another silkworm moth of the opposite sex from a mile away.[1] While our mating instinct may not be as developed as this species, nature has bestowed an exquisite sensitivity upon our romantic radar, programmed to find just the right person to trigger whatever emotional circuitry we need to work through.

Harville Hendrix, the founder of Imago Relationship Therapy, illuminates this phenomenon in a way that sheds new light on our entire intimacy journey. He explains that we are attracted to people who remind us of some of the most important emotional characteristics of our primary caregivers (usually our mother and father). Consciously, we are drawn to the positive qualities of our new love interest, but unconsciously, as Hendrix explains, we are attracted to "someone with the same deficits of care and attention that hurt us in the first place."[2]

Even as adults, all of us have unresolved childhood hurts. Hendrix explains that unconsciously we seek healing through our relationship with our romantic partner. And we try to achieve this healing by bonding with someone who we sense has the potential to cause us pain in similar ways to how we were hurt as children. Unconsciously we hope that this person, by loving us as we need to be loved, will help us come back to an original sense of wholeness and healing.[3]

This also explains why our greatest heartbreaks often occur with our most intense, fiery attractions. Some people react to these past heartbreaks by only dating those on the low end of the spectrum. They are frightened of the intense feelings and the risk of pain when they deal with people on the high end of the attraction scale. They often feel safest with people who don't do much for them on a physical or romantic level because it just feels more comfortable that way. But the downside is usually boredom, frustration, and lack of passion.

Many others only date people on the high end of the spectrum, just going for their iconic types, because they believe that's where real love and passion lie. Usually, a combination of physical characteristics and emotional traits determine our level of attraction. You may think it's because of her red hair and great body—

and it is! But you may also be registering the incredibly subtle curl of her lip that reminds you of your mom, with whom that miniscule curl of the lip would become a snarl of disapproval, leaving you feeling desperate to make her love you again. All of this processing happens beyond our conscious awareness. We just feel the thrill of fear and desire. So with a high-number person, you can tell that you're attracted in a fraction of a second. While this may bring about more excitement (and more drama), it's rarely comfortable or secure.

People who only date in the high-number section of the spectrum are drawn to the immediate charge of adrenaline and lust that comes with dating our iconically "hot" types. The people who date in this way are much more likely to remain single. By contrast, attraction to people who are in the middle of the spectrum is rarely as immediate. It takes more time for you to get a sense of how interested you really are.

If you are willing to date in the middle range of the attraction spectrum, you are much more likely to find real and lasting love than if you only date in the very low or very high range. Dating in the middle range is not a matter of selling out, because immediate attraction isn't the best forecaster of future passion. Intense attractions blind us to the actual quality of our interaction with others, and to the true character of the people we are drawn to. Midrange attractions are less blinding; in these attractions, it is easier to evaluate a person's real personality. And let's not forget that attractions can grow. Many of us have had the experience of having our attraction grow as we get to know someone better.

When we meet people in an environment that sparks insecurity—like most dating events, bars, and clubs—it's easy to fall back into old patterns, like homing in on our iconic types or, conversely, avoiding the people we are really attracted to out of fear of rejection. If we can hold firm to our commitment to avoid attractions of deprivation—no matter how sexy and compelling they may be—and only pursue attractions of inspiration, we can save ourselves vast amounts of pain, and move much more quickly toward the kind of love we really want.

Two very valid questions immediately arise for people when they hear my views about the attraction spectrum. The first question: "Are you suggesting that I settle for someone I'm not attracted to just because he or she is *good for me*?"

My answer: Absolutely not! The point is that attraction can grow based upon connection, something few of us are ever taught. If you've met someone great and your attraction isn't intense yet, I'm suggesting that you create an environment where your attraction can grow—and then see what happens. If your attraction grows, that's wonderful, and if it doesn't, it's simply not a match.

And the second question: "What if I take all the time I need, and the person falls in love with me? There's a good chance I still won't be interested. Is that fair to the other person?"

My answer to this valid and thoughtful concern: It's completely fair if you don't make promises you can't keep, you don't pretend a level of commitment you're not ready for, and if you're honest about the fact you're still in the stage of getting to know him or her. What if this is someone you could really love and you choose not to give things a chance? You'd be cheating this person, and yourself, of a potential future together. Let the other person make his own choice. And let's not forget: in the long run it might turn out that *he* isn't interested in *you*! Only time together will help you both know.

In order for this approach to make sense, it's important to realize that we can grow our attractions. Understanding this concept can save you from the loss of a potentially wonderful relationship. In retrospect, I see that I lost years of happiness because I didn't know—or believe—that attractions could grow. I thought I was selling out on myself and my future by pursuing my less immediately fiery attractions. In fact, the reverse was true. Once you commit to seeking only attractions of inspiration, and once you learn how to grow passion in inspiring relationships, you'll find that your entire dating life changes dramatically.

Moving from Warm Connection to Attraction

As I've cited previously, research has repeatedly proven that intimate interactions such as gentle touch, intimate personal disclosure, acts of kindness, and eye gazing create a sense of connection that can grow into attraction. Attraction can be cultivated, grown, and developed.

People have known this for years. Bonding behaviors can spark romance and intimacy, even when couples aren't initially attracted to each other. Research on arranged marriages has proved the same point. Couples in well-planned arranged marriages tend to grow more in love as time goes on. In nonarranged marriages, it's the reverse. Robert Epstein of Harvard University has studied this phenomenon extensively, interviewing more than a hundred couples in arranged marriages and comparing this information with a wide range of research about love in arranged and nonarranged marriages. His research findings showed that in nonarranged marriages, feelings of love faded by up to 50 percent in eighteen months, while the love in arranged marriages gradually kept growing, and by the five-year point it surpassed the degree of love in nonarranged marriages. After ten years, he found, the love in arranged marriages was on average nearly twice as strong as in nonarranged marriages![4]

It makes sense. Imagine going into an arranged marriage. You know that this person will be your mate for life. Imagine meeting your arranged mate and discovering that she or he is reasonably attractive and intelligent, and treats you really well. Jackpot! You know that your future depends on the effort you put into this relationship. You're not going mess this up—it's your future and this is someone attractive, smart, and kind—so the only choice left is to make it work. And that is what you do.

Now imagine meeting this same person in a normal dating situation. He is attractive, but there are a lot more attractive people out there. He treats you well, but his personality has some quirks, and you wonder if you could do better. Your feelings seem to be growing, but whenever things get rough, you wonder if that means you should look for someone else.

You can see why the love in a well-planned arranged marriage is more likely to grow. The couple is more likely to grow it. They aren't waiting to see how much the love grows on its own. They grow it because their commitment to the relationship is unquestioned.

Exploring Romantic Possibilities When You're Not Sure of Your Attraction

At every point on the attraction spectrum there are pluses and minuses. At each point you will have challenges and opportunities that characterize that particular level of attraction. Knowing these challenges and opportunities will help you when you date people at any point on the spectrum. At some point you might meet someone who feels like an attraction of inspiration but with whom there is only a very small amount of sexual spark. If you decide to explore something romantic with this person, it's really important to be gentle with yourself; allow for the periods where attraction ebbs and flows, and don't become desperate or frightened when your attraction is at low tide. In time, things will become clearer. The attraction will grow—or it won't. During this time you need to use your skills to see whether you can cultivate and develop the physical, emotional, and spiritual connection you have with the person you are dating. If not, it's out of your hands and you have no obligation except to remain decent and kind. But with these tools in hand you don't have to cheat yourself of a love that could grow into something beautiful, secure, and healing.

Remember, in this phase of your dating life you have a right to experience a tasting menu of healthy connections. You have the right to meet new people and experience new kinds of attractions—and those attractions can come in all shapes and forms—without the pressure to commit, the pressure to have sex, or the pressure to give more than you want to give. When you realize that attraction can grow through connection, you'll have so many more options to find healthy love. As always, don't put pressure on yourself. Your desire for sexual attraction doesn't make you a superficial person. Just let the human connection deepen at its own pace, and allow room for attraction to develop.

DEEPENING SEXUAL DESIRE
AND ROMANTIC PASSION

What do we do when we meet someone who inspires us and we feel attraction, but not enough to fall in love? Or perhaps we are already attracted to someone, but we want to move our attraction to a deeper level. First, we celebrate our luck in meeting this person. Next, we exercise that spark.

When you build muscle through exercise, your body creates new capillaries to feed that muscle. When you create new love, something similar happens. New neural pathways, emotional pathways, new rituals, sense memories, and needs get created. As you start to care more deeply about someone, invisible tendrils begin to grow in your thinking, in your sexual imaginings and longings, in your growing sense of dependence on him. Your psyche, your sexuality, and your heart begin to create attachment to that person, to make him your own. You become specialized in him in so many ways. Sharing parts of yourself that are ever closer to the center of your being is a powerful way to build love. If you can share those tender parts of yourself and feel heard and appreciated, you may well feel love deepening. Here is a simple rule to build the love in almost any relationship: give more fully, and receive more openly. This wonderful instruction applies to sex as well. Receptivity and generosity deepen love in a powerful way.

Janet met Patricia at her best friend's wedding, and they grew to care about each other deeply. A few months into the relationship Patricia contracted pneumonia and was quite ill for a period of weeks. Janet recalls a telling moment. It was a sunny day and Patricia was lying in her bed. Janet had just brought her a glass of cold water with a straw and held the water for her, stroking her hair. Patricia was embarrassed because she was in her bathrobe and hadn't washed her hair for a few days. She felt disheveled and unattractive. She had no makeup on and she was looking gaunt and pale. Janet remembers this moment clearly. She remembers the sunlight hitting Patricia's face and how it felt to stroke her hair. And, as she cared for Patricia, she found that she was becoming very sexually aroused. She felt like she was swooning with a mix of desire and love, and she realized clearly how much she cared about her partner. It was on that day, when Patricia felt so embarrassed about her appearance, that Janet knew for sure that she had fallen in love. She told me years later that she never forgot that defining moment. In some relationships, it can take time for our attraction to build. In those cases, it can be difficult to stay, to resist fleeing in search of something more clear-cut. As a result of our tendency to flee from this period of uncertainty, many potentially wonderful relationships get cut off before ever being given a chance. The truth is that we can deepen our healthy attractions, and we can intensify the passion in those attractions. In a healthy relationship, the more we focus on the things that trigger our desire, the more our passion can build. The researcher and author Elaine Aron writes, "Research shows that the longer you contemplate an object in an emotional way, the more intense the emotions toward that object will become ... [T]he simple message here is that the more you contemplate someone you feel you could love, the more you will indeed love that person."[5]

When you are growing love and attraction, try to disengage from a sense of inner pressure and obligation. No matter how wonderful the person, *you're not obligated to be more attracted to him or her than you are.* Forcing your feelings will block the possibility of a natural flow of attraction. Instead, allow yourself to reflect on what attracts you to her, what turns you on, and what you appreciate. What parts of her personality and your interactions gratify you emotionally? Let yourself name those and engage them even more. What interests and passions do you have in common? Research also proves that engaging in novel activities (particularly ones that hold a sense of heightened arousal and risk) build attraction and intimacy between members of a couple.[6]

Think physically, too. What parts of her body attract you? What would you like to do with those parts? Take time to let your fantasies unfurl. You might simply want to hold hands at the movies, or to kiss, or to just gently touch lips for a long time. You might desire to touch and caress a part of your partner's body, or have your partner do the same to you. You might imagine quick, hot sex; long, lazy sex; a kinky fantasy; anything. Honor whatever you're imagining. You may never act on it, and that's fine. This kind of sexual imagining is one way we can grow our passion. If you want to begin to explore an actual sexual relationship, then you can follow your sense of desire for your new love interest and ask for what you want—and no more. I advise against having full sex for at least the first five or six dates. When we desire someone but still postpone the sex, surprising new pathways of attraction form. It's a great way to grow passion. Conversely, having sex too early often makes us want to flee. So go slowly on the outside, but allow yourself free rein in your fantasy life.

If your desire is more sensual than sexual, that's fine too. My client Tina met Roberto in New York when he was visiting from Italy. She knew she liked him, but she wasn't attracted enough to desire sex with him. She just wanted to cuddle and for them to hold each other. He invited her to visit him in Italy, but she wasn't sure if she should make the trip. Speaking to her learning partner, she said, "I don't know if I should go all the way to Europe just to cuddle with someone." Her wise friend replied, "Really? I can't think of a *better* reason to go to Europe!" My client decided to take the trip, and over time she and Roberto fell deeply in love. She was wise enough to take all the time she needed, and he was wise enough to let her.

There's another benefit to nonsexual touching. In the words of Craig Malkin, professor of psychology at Harvard University, "Multiple lines of evidence confirm the romantic importance of oxytocin, the 'cuddle hormone,' which is released in greater quantities when we touch our loved ones. *The more you touch, the more oxytocin is released, which helps create feelings of closeness and trust—which leads to more touch.* It's a positive intimacy loop."[7]

MICRO-MEDITATION

Seeing the Beauty | Two minutes

The world is filled with myriad aspects of beauty, and you can enjoy them commitment-free! Try this lovely meditation at any time you want. I encourage you to try it on a date with someone you like. When you see or are with someone you are attracted to on any level, just allow yourself to deepen into the attraction. Allow yourself to focus on the emotional, behavioral, and physical aspects that are desirable to you. You might like someone's legs, someone's laugh, or his arms, lips, or voice. The way she moves, or the way she smiles. Allow yourself to sink into the pleasure of that attraction with absolutely no sense of obligation or demand. Don't feel that you have to make your attraction any bigger than it is. And then simply move on, enriched by the appreciation, longing, and humanity you allowed yourself to feel.

Note: There are a few caveats to be aware of with this deeply evocative micro-meditation. If you wrestle with issues of sexual compulsion, I advise you not to do this exercise without appropriate support—it can be very "triggering." And I encourage readers to only do it with people who are appropriate (for example, not your best friend's wife!).

Carolyn first got to know Richie when he started working at his dad's local pizza place. She was fourteen and he was twenty-one; romance wasn't even a consideration. As the years went by they became very close friends. Richie desired a closer relationship with

Carolyn, but he never pushed himself on her, and so they remained only friends. When she decided to marry her boyfriend, she told him the big news. Richie listened and said, ruefully, "Don't do that!" but she didn't take him seriously. Carolyn went ahead and got married and had two daughters with her husband, but the marriage wasn't good at all. When they separated, her former husband barely helped her and the girls. She moved back in with her mother, and it was a very challenging time. The Carolyn of today is a kind, gracious, and loving person, but she said to me, "You wouldn't have recognized me, Ken. I was angry and bitter—broke, overwhelmed, and wound up tight."

All through that time, Richie remained a caring presence in her life. He babysat the girls a few nights a week so she could go to school. He took them all on fun day trips. He was a regular and happy part of their life, and he always took the time to make sure that Carolyn and the girls were okay. Over the course of a few years, Carolyn realized she was falling deeply in love with him. The sex didn't come first—in fact, it took time for that part of the relationship to develop. Even though she had always found him attractive, she had just never thought of him in that way. Until she began to fall in love. "My love for Richie was so complete that sex just became a part of it," she later said. "It was never really separate. Once I began falling in love with the man he is, he became more and more physically desirable to me." I've known them both for years, and their love is obvious, warm, and solid. Their happiness is palpable.

Carolyn went on to say, "Culture makes us go for the physical first. There are so many people who might have so much to offer, but you might not even have turned your head to look at them because they aren't your type. But really, it's the whole person you really fall in love with. When you let yourself fall in love with the whole person, the potential is so much greater."

Carolyn's words carry the richness of hard-won wisdom: "Let yourself fall in love with the whole person. The physical will often come naturally when you let the full person in."

FOCUSING ON WHAT MOVES YOU
AND TURNS YOU ON

Simply following our emotional and sexual feelings of connection and desire can help our attractions to grow. We may be on a date and simply want to hold hands, nothing more. We should let ourselves do just that. When we do, we may feel something. Perhaps warmth, perhaps fondness, perhaps a sexual frisson. Feeling that pleasure, pressure-free, allows the possibility of more — if that suits us. We may want to brush our hands against her nipples through her dress, or rest our hand high up on his thigh, close to his crotch. Or perhaps we just want to look into his eyes, or cuddle, or be quiet together. Or we may want to get really wild. On a date with someone in the middle range of attraction, we can ask ourselves what we'd want to do with her. This is an adventure, and every connection will have its unique chemistry. If this is a relationship that has real romantic potential, we will find that our desire is increasing, because we are following the unique sensual and sexual connection we have with this person.

Let's say you're only somewhat attracted to your partner, but certain of his physical and emotional traits really turn you on. Let yourself focus on these physical or emotional turn-ons, such as your partner's voice, a body part, or a personality attribute. Enjoy them, deepen into them. If any of these fantasies have heat and traction for you, try them out in your own exploratory masturbations, if that's something you like to do. The key here is to explore what you want to explore, and don't do anything you don't want to do. Do the same with your emotional connection. Perhaps you notice that when he talks about his dog, his quality of affection comes through, and you find that really attractive. Go with it. Ask him questions about his dog, spend time with the two of them, and let your pleasure and sense of connection keep growing.

Remember Ann, our friend in chapter 4 who was only attracted to arrogant guys? Let's take a look at what happened for her as she explored these ideas.

Ann met Steve at a local independent cinema club that she had just joined. Steve seemed like a great guy and she found him attractive enough to flirt with and get to know, and finally to go on a date with.

Their first date was rough for her. She didn't like what he was wearing and she didn't like his haircut, and overall she didn't feel particularly attracted to him. In her old days she would have done her best to get right out of Dodge. Now she was open to trying something different. She knew he was a nice guy, and she was attracted to him when she first met him. By the end of the date she was confused. It was still a gray area for her. But I reminded her of what my mentor John McNeill once said to me: "If you're not sure that you're attracted to someone, keep dating him. If it's the right match, in time he will start to become more beautiful to you."

The second date was a relief. She found him more attractive. But she was still worried that she was wasting her time and his. Yet the quality of the conversation was wonderful. And the things he said about his two young daughters and the volunteer work he did with abused animals completely won her over. She found that she wanted to rest her hand on his, and she did so. There was a wonderful warm feeling, though no serious sexual sparks, and she kept her hand there.

Later on in the meal she noticed his handsome hairy forearms, something she really liked in a guy. And she began to feel slightly sexually attracted to him.

A few days later they were on the phone. She was lying on the couch and found to her great surprise that she was becoming sexually aroused simply by hearing his rich-toned voice. She was thrilled because she was liking him more and more. Knowing that the sexual attraction was growing along with their intimacy was a wonderful feeling for her, and a completely new experience.

Over the next five or six dates she learned to relax and trust her feelings. When she wasn't attracted she didn't push herself to do anything physical. When she wanted to do something physical with him she was bold and allowed herself to take that risk. She told him clearly that she needed to go very slowly. Over a long period of time, things gradually smoothed out. She found that she was mostly always attracted to him, and that her attraction would often spike to thrilling levels when their connection was strong. She had found someone truly wonderful, and she couldn't believe her good fortune.

Once again, let me remind you: Pressure to love can extinguish new love quickly. If you try the suggestions for growing connection, and sexual or romantic desire doesn't grow, please don't beat yourself up. Sexual attraction can't be forced. By trying these methods, you'll give the spark a chance to develop. That's all you can do. If the spark doesn't ignite or grow over time, don't blame yourself or pressure yourself. This is about giving yourself the liberty to connect in new ways.

YOUR SEXUAL SOUL AND SEXUAL CORE GIFTS

Each of us has sexual gifts as well as emotional ones. We also have wounds that intersect with those gifts. What blocks us from knowing our sexual gifts? What can we do to claim them in our lives and our relationships?

As terribly as we've been trained around dating, our training around sex has been even worse! Few of us have been taught how to handle our lusty sexual exuberance and our secret sexual desires in a healthy, nondestructive way. And few of us have been taught how to use sex to share our deepest tenderness, our very soul. And, God knows, almost none of us has been taught how to embrace both parts simultaneously.

The great majority of us come to a compromise. We don't let ourselves go all the way with our tenderness or all the way with our lusty desires during sex with the one we love. When we show one side it's often hard to show the other at the same time. All of us fall into sexual patterns where we enjoy sex without touching the heart of our deepest vulnerability and desire. Most of us, deep down, are both wilder and more tender than we allow ourselves to reveal.

We need to allow ourselves some wildness in our sex. Sexual attraction has been described as "a spark that needs to jump a gap." When we avoid risk by not sharing what we want and need, nor asking the same of our partner, we diminish the intimacy between ourselves and our loved one. In the long run, it hurts our relationship when we give up our deep authenticity to keep things safe with our partner. That is when sex becomes bland, when we begin to either shut down sexually or start fantasizing about an affair. When experimentation dies, Eros dies along with it. Bring Eros into the relationship as much as you can. That means sharing with your partner the things in sex that move you most deeply, that turn you on most intensely. It means listening for the same with your partner, and moving step by step together to the sexual soul of your relationship.

EXPRESSION OF HIDDEN
SEXUAL/EMOTIONAL/ROMANTIC DESIRES

Sigmund Freud coined the phrase *Madonna-whore complex*. This is how he described this painful yet familiar syndrome wherein sex and intimacy can't coexist: "Where such men love they have no desire and where they desire they cannot love."[8]

In relation to both the word *Madonna* and the word *whore*, my response is the same: "You say that like it's a bad thing. Well, it's not."

Most of us have the need to see our partner as pure, above the kind of sex that objectifies us and him. Perhaps above the physical completely. And most of us, male or female, have the need for the whore as well, where we surrender to wild, sticky, messy sex. Where we can take risks and allow ourselves to submit and be submitted to. Wild sex, mixed with love and an almost nonsexual adoration, is a kind of paradise.

How do you get through the difficult and culturally induced

dichotomization of Madonna and whore, or sexuality and spirituality? By gradually developing a healthy relationship with both parts.

Where you are spiritually moved by your partner's kindness,
goodness, and innocence, cherish that. Go with it. Feel your feelings of love and valuing and protectiveness. When you feel lustful,
share that with an open heart too. Practice holding both. That's
where richer love comes into fruition.

TWO QUESTIONS TO DISCOVER
YOUR SEXUAL CORE GIFTS

There are two wonderful focus questions that can serve to deepen
your entire sexual and romantic experience. They are simple
questions—in fact, they are obvious. They are also gentle, yet like so
many gentle things, they have the power to change us deeply. Perhaps this is why we spend so much time avoiding them.

Question 1: What Turns You On Most in Sex?

Frequently our sexual turn-ons just don't fit our self-image. We
might fantasize about being sexually submissive, but feel humiliated by that desire. Or we might fantasize about being sexually
dominant, but feel afraid of who that makes us into. Perhaps the
things that truly excite us are embarrassing because they are so
"vanilla"—so uninventive and basic. Whether exotic or not, our deepest erotic sparks are portals to a deeper experience of sex and of self.

Often these sexual portals illumine parts of ourselves we just
don't know what do with. Few of us have been taught how to handle our most evocative sexual fantasies in a creative, celebratory,
nondestructive way. We may judge our most colorful desires as odd,
even perverted.

The theater director and lyricist David Schechter rescues the
word *perverse* by proposing a lovely twist to it. Schechter asks,
"What if perverse means 'per-verse'—or, 'through poetry'?" When

we explore our wild side, we play in a landscape of sexual poetry, a world of inner symbolism that may never make conscious sense but still feels gratifying and meaningful. The majority of us need help in embracing our wild side in sex, and in distinguishing between behaviors that are harmful to us or our partner and those that are simply, and wonderfully, "per-verse." Take a moment to think what kinds of sex excite you most. What actions, what body parts, what behaviors—what outfits?

Allow yourself the freedom of play in your reflections. You will probably hit some waves of discomfort as you go. Track them; if they are too disturbing, it may be best to enlist the support of a skilled, credentialed, and nonjudgmental psychotherapist. If your fantasies just feel embarrassing, surprising, or beyond the pale, see if you can imagine embracing them. Whatever they are, I assure you that there are others who share the same turn-ons, and with whom sharing those desires would be an experience of mutual delight. Your future partner has hidden desires of his or her own. Following our own deeper turn-ons, including ones we have been timid about exploring, can help deepen and enrich our entire sexual experience.

John was always sexually in control in his past relationships with women. He loved to be the giver of pleasure, and felt it suited him. Unfortunately these relationships continually fell into patterns where he was doing all the giving. He was the generous one, the patient one, the one who gave and directed things. As he learned to follow his attractions of inspiration and value his gifts, he noticed that he could now become sexually attracted to much stronger women, who previously weren't his type. He had been dating Caitlyn, a very self-assured woman, for about three months and their connection was quickly deepening. Suddenly he found that he was fantasizing about her sexually in a new way. He wanted to be "taken," to release control and give it over. If he was really honest, he wanted to be dominated. The thought of being submissive was very exciting. It turns out that Caitlyn was delighted and intrigued by his new fantasies. In their now-blossoming relationship, he explored this sexual dimension of his being, and as he did, his attraction to Caitlyn deepened more and more. In time, as his love grew, he found he loved both roles, and a fluid shifting between roles became a delightful sexual secret they shared.

Question 2: What Touches You Most Deeply in Sex?

This is a marvelous question, and one that every sexual adult should enjoy, relish, and reflect upon. Interestingly, it often leaves us feeling even more vulnerable than the previous one.

Have you ever been emotionally touched during sex in a way that took you by surprise? What happened to create that experience? Try to think back and remember. It will tell you worlds about who you are and your deepest sexual gifts.

Are there parts of your body that, when touched in a certain way, trigger deep emotions? Is there a pacing in sex that touches and moves you deeply? If you are partnered, what touches your partner most deeply in sex?

When Kris and her now-husband first had sex, he did something that felt odd to her. In the middle of enthusiastic sex, he began to slow down, and then stopped moving altogether. He wrapped her in his arms as he lay on top of her, and then — lay perfectly still. She assumed he hadn't climaxed, so she was bewildered, but she went with the moment. As they lay motionless in their embrace, she felt something begin to shake inside her. Out of nowhere, she began to weep. They clung together, neither knowing what had hit them. Sometimes this beautiful ritual would happen spontaneously during their lovemaking and it became a hallmark of many episodes of their sexual expression throughout the years.

In sex and in life, many of us are both wilder and more tender than we may feel comfortable with. Both our wildness and our tenderness are portals to our deepest self and our richer expression of ourselves in the world. You can ask yourself these two questions during sex as a way to guide you and your partner to those portals of intimacy: What expressions would touch me and my partner most deeply on an emotional level? How can we follow the trail of our deep turn-ons in this moment?

In expressing your deeper and more hidden sexual desires, there is the opportunity for thrill, deep connection, joyful intimacy—and lots of emotional discomfort. Remember to maintain a warm connection to the person you're with. It might be difficult to do that when you're feeling discomfort about the new behaviors that you're trying. If you and your partner can talk about these feelings, if you can still enjoy each other, and if you can maintain affection, warmth, and eye contact, in most cases you will feel your discomfort begin to lift.

DISCOVERING YOUR SEXUAL AND ROMANTIC CORE GIFT

Take some quiet, relaxed time with your journal for this important process. Answer each question from the heart, feeling your feelings and not censoring what you write.

1. Have you ever had the feeling of lust and intimate love fused together? When sexually touching your partner, have you ever felt like you were touching his or her heart? Remember how you felt. If you haven't yet experienced this, just imagine what it would be like. The experience of sex fused with intimacy, whether you just imagined it or have experienced it in real life, captures one of your most central sexual Core Gifts. It is your portal place—a place where you can connect to your sexual magic. In this place, your sexuality and your heart befriend each other.

2. What words capture how you feel when sexual desire and intimate love join together for you?

3. What is an image, a piece of art or music, or any other thing that captures the above feeling?

4. Do you suppress this gift in your sexual and romantic life? How do you do this?

5. What kind of sex deprives this gift of oxygen? What does it feel like for you when that happens?

6. In your past sex life, has there ever been someone with whom you have felt safe revealing this part of yourself? If so, just take a moment to appreciate that memory.

7. Name or describe your sexual and romantic Core Gift in one or more sentences. See if you can put words on this capacity for feeling both deep intimacy and real sexual passion. If you haven't experienced it but can imagine it, that is good enough.

8. Allow yourself to picture being in a relationship with someone you love, freely sharing this Core Gift and receiving the same back from your partner. Describe how that would feel. Take a moment to relish that thought.

Each of us has sexual and romantic Core Gifts, and it is a life journey to discover them. I hope you look for this and work toward it in your next relationship. You can ask yourself what kinds of touch, pacing, sexual actions, feelings, and eye contact would allow this state. The more you know the answers to such questions, the more you will be able to have access to that wonderful experience. Your sexual and romantic Core Gift is about much more than technique, position, or particular sexual activities. It is an invitation to love, shared joy, and intimacy. It deserves to be celebrated.

Deeper Dating Workbook

PERSONAL EXERCISE

Your Sexual Journey

Think of a few of the people in your life who have taught you good and important things on your sexual journey. Reflect on what these people taught you and take a moment to appreciate each person.

LEARNING PARTNER EXERCISES

Do the following field trips with your learning partner. If that is not possible, just share your experiences and reflections together when you have both completed each field trip.

Deeper Dating Field Trip 1:
Your Intense Attractions

This exercise requires you to go to an event with a good number of single people. It can be done alone, but it's more helpful to do it with your learning partner or a safe friend.

For the first part of your exercise focus on the people you're extremely attracted to. Just notice them. Don't do anything about it—yet. Note the physical attributes that attract you the most. Now take the time to go a bit deeper. Watch these people as they interact with others. What does their body language convey? What kind of presence do they project?

After you've done this for a while meet up with your partner. Point out to each other the people you have been observing. Allow your partner to describe the quality of their presence: warm, cool, superficial, angry, intelligent, playful. Then do the same for your learning partner. When it comes to intense attractions, we need to assume that our intuition may well be impaired. Your learning partner's feedback might be very telling.

Are there any extremely attractive people who seem to have qualities of inspiration? If so, try to speak with them. You may need your learning partner to encourage and coach you. For many of us, approaching extremely attractive people can be scary.

Afterward, go to a café together with your friend. Do a postmortem about what you noticed about your patterns, and share feedback, laughter, and insights. There's no reason for this journey not to be fun!

Deeper Dating Field Trip 2:
Your Middle-Range Attractions

Go to another event where there are a good number of single people. This time, focus on your middle-range attractions: people to whom you are somewhat attracted but not overwhelmingly so.

Without pressure, let yourself enjoy the process of seeing these subtler attractions emerge. These may be people you never would have focused on in the past. Keep watching and noting your reactions. Do any of them seem kind, funny, warm, emotionally present?

Now you are using your emotional intuition to choose who interests you instead of only focusing on the physical turn-on. Are any of them starting to look sexy to you? Let yourself fantasize: "This one I'd like to kiss. That one I'd love to see with his or her shirt off." Use the "Seeing the Beauty" micro-meditation (page 213) and enjoy your fantasies. Do any of these people seem like they might be attractions of inspiration? Try to talk with them. If any have potential, exchange numbers. Be open to new friendships as well.

After you leave, go somewhere with your learning partner or friend and share insights and experiences. If you couldn't go with your learning partner, share your experiences when you speak. What did you notice about this experience? What felt new and different for you? What did you learn? And of course, did you meet anyone interesting? If not, no worries. These field trips are about learning. Keep practicing these skills and you will definitely meet people with real potential.

12

Being Loved into Fullness

We are born in relationship, we are wounded in relationship, and we can be healed in relationship. Indeed, we cannot be fully healed outside of a relationship.

—HARVILLE HENDRIX,
Getting the Love You Want: A Guide for Couples

Years ago I took the opportunity to hike a small portion of the Appalachian Trail. It was a wonderful adventure, but what I remember most of all was that we kept losing track of the trail. It looked pretty easy on the map, but the map didn't show the fallen trees that took us off course, the river with no means to cross it, and all the confusing paths leading in different directions. Thank God for the markers and milestones that pointed us back to the trail or proved to us that we were still on it. Each time we found a marker, we were reassured.

I imagine that over the course of this book your intimacy journey has felt not too different from my hiking experience. My assumption is that you've hit many difficult points and "dating emergencies" that this book didn't even cover, and that many times the techniques didn't work as well as you had hoped. But I'm also guessing that you too have found wonderful, important markers and milestones telling you that the tools you're learning *do* work, and that your gifts *can* guide you to intimacy. Those "marker moments" of finding the trail are so important. At those times, we feel safe in the knowledge that the path we're taking is right, simply because it follows the contours of our authentic self. Can you remember a few of your own personal markers—moments of insight, growth, and understanding that felt important to you?

Your search for a loving partner matters greatly, but equally important is the work you've done to *practice* love. In the last months, you have changed the question from "How do I rate in love" to "Can I be brave enough to treasure my most intimate self, generous enough to share it, and wise enough to choose the right people?" And with these questions, everything changes.

Godfrey Minot Camille was a participant of the Grant Study, one of the most comprehensive longitudinal studies of human development ever undertaken.[1] His entire life history was tracked from his years in college until his death in his eighties.

Camille was born to parents who were cold, suspicious, and unloving. In Camille's words, "Before there were dysfunctional families, I came from one." Until he was thirty-five, Camille was deeply hypochondriacal, and extremely manipulative in his attempts to use his "symptoms" to get attention. He attempted suicide after graduation from medical school, but survived the experience. The Grant Study researchers felt that he was one of the least likely to ever build a happy, successful life.

Then, when he was thirty-five, he had a life-changing experience. He was hospitalized for fourteen months with pulmonary tuberculosis. His illness, this time, was a real one. And in that year, for the first time in his life, he was cared for, listened to, and treated as though he mattered. Those fourteen months of attention and care were enough to heal many of his lifelong wounds. His hunger to be *recognized* was finally met in this most unexpected way. That period changed the course of his entire life. Camille felt his time in the hospital was almost like a religious rebirth. "Someone with a capital S cared about me," he wrote. "Nothing has been so tough since that year in the sack."

When he was released from the hospital, Camille went into what the study called a "developmental explosion that went on for thirty years." He had a spiritual awakening that remained with him his whole life. He became a caring and successful physician. He fell in love, got married, and had two children. He created a life full of love and giving—the kind of life he had always wanted. He entered two psychoanalyses. He went mountain climbing in the Alps. He became someone who could *give*.

When Camille was almost seventy, his Grant interviewer asked him what he had learned from his children. "You know what I learned from my children?" he blurted out, tears in his eyes. "I learned love!" The interviewer recounted, "Many years later, having seized a serendipitous opportunity to interview his daughter, I believed him. I have interviewed many Grant Study children, but this woman's love for her father remains the most stunning that I have encountered among them."

When he was seventy-five, Camille described how love had healed him: "[T]he truly gratifying unfolding has been into the person I've slowly become: comfortable, joyful, connected, and effective. Since it wasn't widely available then, I hadn't read that children's classic *The Velveteen Rabbit*, which tells how connectedness is something we must let happen to us, and then we become solid and whole. As that tale recounts tenderly, only love can make us real."

Looking at the arc of Camille's life, we can see that his intense suffering and his great happiness sprang from the same Core Gift: an enormous capacity for love. This gift was so powerful that the lack of love in his life almost killed him. But in an environment filled with attention and connection, his genius was finally liberated. Camille was most wounded at the very place where he was most gifted, but the love in his adult life was able to heal many of those wounds.

In your past relationships of deprivation, you too may have felt a terrible yet somehow familiar pain—the pain of the parts of you that were never truly honored or embraced. The place in you where you have felt weakest and most ashamed is the site of a gift in you that was not honored enough to unfold fully. When a vulnerable and precious part of us is not appreciated, we experience it as a weakness or a wound, not as a gift.

However, when we feel that our gifts are honored, we experience an innate sense of worth and of love. Our most essential wounds reveal the secret that was inside them all along—a gift that had never been loved into fullness. We may not have the opportunity to be cared for during fourteen months in a sanatorium, but we can find our own places of healing. We can create our own "developmental explosion" by embracing and befriending our Core Gifts, by following our own Guiding Insights, and by sharing our intimate self with the precious people who treasure us for who we are. As you do this, you may one day look back on your attractions of deprivation and see that the pain they caused led you to reclaim your own gifts, that these relationships were like a birth canal toward your own realization, a passageway for you to claim your orphaned gifts and help them come back into the world. Relationships that end in pain are often the very things that lead us back to our gifts. *Behind our defenses are our hurts. Behind our hurts are our gifts. And in the heart of our gifts, we find a portal to love.*

Let me offer you one more tool, some words of guidance and wisdom from a very special person: the future you.

MICRO-MEDITATION

A Message for You | Three minutes

Think back over the last months and see if you can pick the lesson or insight that had the most meaning for you in this course. Take a moment to reflect on why this insight means so much to you.

Now imagine yourself down the road a few years, having learned to live this insight much more fully. Imagine who you will become as you embody this lesson in deeper ways. Picture this more loving, wiser you. What does your face look like? What do your eyes reflect? Feel what it is like to look into the eyes of this wiser you.

Now, let your future self tell you whatever message he or she wishes to share with you. Allow yourself to drink in that message. Let your wiser self also tell you what he or she needs from you. Take a moment to let this request sink in. See if you have a response. Thank your future self, and ask if you can keep meeting in the future.

Take a few moments to sit with your feelings, and to feel the ripples of what you just did.

It turns out there *is* a brass ring, but you don't have to compete for it. It's yours already. The brass ring is your own deep humanity—and the relationships in which you feel treasured. No matter what you've been told, no matter what you've feared to be true, your search for love is not a race against time. It is not a hunt for a needle in the haystack. You are on a much greater journey than that. You are learning love by finding its source within you. Every insight you gain moves you closer to your goal of a wonderful life partner.

You can do this. You have the tools you need. You have the gifts that lie in the core of your heart, and you have learned to treasure their humanity and their promise. In the long run, it is the act of treasuring and the sense of being treasured that makes all the difference in the world. Trust in your gifts; they will lead you to love. It's a promise.

Deeper Dating Workbook

PERSONAL EXERCISE

A Message for You

For this process you'll need an envelope, a stamp, and a piece of letter paper. Take out your paper and write a letter from the heart—to yourself. Include three things in this letter:

1. What you appreciate about yourself.

2. Whatever thoughts and guidance you want to share with yourself as a reminder.

3. The message you got from your more evolved self in the "A Message for You" micro-meditation visualization (above).

Place the letter in the envelope. Address it to yourself, stamp it, and mail it, or give it to a friend or your learning partner to mail at an unknown time.

LEARNING PARTNER EXERCISES

This is your last formal set of learning partner exercises in the book, but that doesn't mean you can't keep working together. Both of you have invested significant time in your work together and hours of learning about yourselves and each other. I strongly encourage you to keep meeting if you wish to. You can redo the whole course, or chapters that felt particularly important to you. And if you live near each other, a great celebration meal might be in order!

Who You Are Becoming

Share your experience and insight around the micro-meditation with your learning partner.

Gift Circle with Your Learning Partner

This wonderful closure process is a great way to end this chapter. Follow the format of the Gift Circle and give each other the positive feedback that is suggested. You'll love the experience—and you both most certainly deserve it.

Afterword

Beyond Deeper Dating

Forget your perfect offering. There is a crack in everything. That's how the light gets in.

—LEONARD COHEN

As you continue your Deeper Dating journey I hope you have a new sense of hope. I hope you have come to believe that you can lead with your deepest self, not hide it until you've sealed the deal. I hope you've met new and wonderful people—but also that you've rediscovered some of the relationships of inspiration that are already in your life. Most of all, I hope you feel as though you are embracing your own lessons of intimacy and working to build a life full of the love you so deserve.

I wish I could be a fly on the wall and watch your moments of bravery, those defining moments in your dating life when you choose self-love over self-doubt, when you stretch your boundaries in a healthy way, when you decide to lead with the ardent humanity of your gifts.

I wish I could watch as you walk away from unkind, unavailable people, witness your bravery as you take a risk with someone you care about, and then see the peace in your face when your risk is honored. I wish I could see the moments when you decide to honor the always imperfect, endlessly human passion in your core, because that is exactly what will lead you to the love you want.

You began this journey with a micro-meditation in which you

imagined being sent off on this Deeper Dating journey by the people who care about you most. Now, in our last micro-meditation, let's revisit that experience.

MICRO-MEDITATION

A Closing Gift | Four minutes

Over the last few months, in your Deeper Dating learning journey, you've built a more loving relationship with your Core Gifts, and you've practiced sharing your gifts with bravery and generosity with the right people. Congratulate yourself for what you've done.

Now take a moment to think of the people who visited you in your first micro-meditation—the people who have loved you most and who want you to find real love. They may be alive or not, but they are still close to your heart. Take a moment to picture each of these precious people. Would any of them have something to say to you now as you finish this course? Visualize their faces as you imagine what each of them might say to you, and allow yourself to be touched by their message to you. Thank them for all their support in your life. Let yourself feel surrounded by everyone's affection. Take a gentle breath in. Exhale and let it all go and slowly open your eyes. Feel the ripples of this micro-meditation in your heart and body.

Know that you are on your way, and that this path, never finished and never perfectly done, is the path of your intimacy journey.

During my many single years, people would tell me that I didn't really want a relationship. If I had really wanted one, I wouldn't have been single for so long. They were so wrong. The pain of my longing was as real as it could be. I did want love. But I was fleeing it at the same time. No one had taught me how to move past my personal minefields and fears. Or how to avoid the paths to disaster carved out for me by popular culture, which led me to look for love without the tools to build it. I'm so thankful that I learned that embracing the parts of myself I had been so uncertain about would finally lead me to love.

In every significant area of your life—your intimate relationships, your creativity, your spiritual life, and your career—it is your Core Gifts that point the way to meaning and love. There's a wisdom inside you that supersedes all the myriad limitations in your life. In your gifts lies your true nature, far wilder, more gentle, and more magnificent than your understanding could ever hope to encompass.

When I think about what it's like to live without our gifts being recognized, I think of Helen Keller as a child, and about the lives of other deaf-blind children. Keller had a vast, loving heart and a fierce intelligence, but her pain must have been endless—trapped in a dark and soundless world with no language, no way to reach or be reached by those who loved her. Her rage and despair made her desperate. But Annie Sullivan saw her gifts, understood her fury at being caged in soundless isolation. Annie gave Helen a bridge to the world by giving her a way to communicate her despair and her longings. Sullivan taught Helen to understand letters, and then words, by pressing their form into the palm of Helen's hand. Helen called Annie "teacher" for the rest of her life.

Like Helen Keller, each of us has gifts that have lived in painful isolation, that were misunderstood or used by others, gifts that we've judged to be flaws. As we've made our way through life, we've protected ourselves by trying to mold those gifts into something more acceptable. Now it's our job, with the help of those who love us, to rescue the core self inside us. To press spelled words of hope and encouragement into the palm of its hands again and again, as Annie Sullivan did for Helen, until we realize that we can reach out across the loneliness that surrounds us and speak in our own language. And when we find those precious people who understand our gifts—not all of them, but the ones that matter most—they find a home. Our true gifts are the path to fulfillment. And they are calling to us all the time.

The reclamation of your gifts will transform your search for love. Every time you choose your soul over your "shoulds" you'll become more powerful. You will start to sense a kind of magic inside you—scary and challenging, yes, but magic all the same. If you've ever been hiking, you've seen that the landscape becomes more lush and more alive as you move closer to a river. It is the same in our lives. Move toward your own river. That is where you will find love. The gifts you've sensed and begun to love during the past months are your river, your fierce and tender path to love.

Your precious gifts hold the power to guide your whole world, and they will lead you to true intimacy, because that is what they are built to do. It all comes down to this magnificent message: Follow the call of your core.

May you have a grand adventure!

Acknowledgments

As a new writer filled with exciting, half-formed ideas, I was blessed with a huge amount of mentorship and support. This book didn't take a village to get finished; it took a small city.

My friend Jonathan Vatner started me off as a new writer. His patience, literary elegance, and gentle but razor-sharp insight shaped this book, and his faith in me is what launched my writing. Mel White, mentor, literary father figure and friend, amazing racer, and true world changer, I cannot thank you enough—with your help, I came to trust myself as a writer. I'm honored to have been your student and privileged to be your friend. Nathaniel Altman, thank you for your invaluable help. Hara Marano, in so many ways you and *Psychology Today* made all this possible for me. Thank you for being a mentor and a friend. Sharon Cohen-Powers, dear friend, thank you for your coaching, your support, and your fierce commitment to my work and its clarity. Some of the key concepts of this book would never have come through without your help. David Greenan, our profound friendship, your constant support, and your wise insights around Gift Theory and intimacy have meant the world to me. Patricia Simko, thank you for our treasured friendship, for your crisp editing, and for the many talks in which you helped me develop the concept of Gift Theory. Julie Williams, my world is a much better place because of you, Mark, and Charlie. I can't thank you enough for your painless, wise, and encouraging editing help. You are extraordinarily gifted. Pam Cytrynbaum, I can't tell you how much I appreciate your friendship, heartfelt support, and save-the-day edits. Arielle Ford, joyful, wise, and generous thought leader, you've been a true "angel" to me in this journey, and I'm so thankful to know you. Arianne Cohen, thank you so much for your incredible support throughout the years. Ross Anderson, John Salvato, Krissy Gasbarre, and Kathryn Janus, you've been angels to me as well—thank you!

Arielle Ford, Thich Nhat Hanh, Harville Hendrix, Helen LaKelly Hunt, Marianne Williamson, Chip Conley, Gay Hendricks, Keith Ferrazzi, Judith Orloff, Arthur Aron, and Eli Finkel, none of you had to take a moment out of your busy schedule and brilliant work to support this project—yet each one of you did. I am so grateful.

Thank you, Cliff Boro, for your generous heartfelt support, and Tom Pace, Dan Negroni, and Brian Burt, for helping move Deeper Dating to the next level.

To all who read and critiqued this manuscript—Greg Romer, Ruth Litman, Maya Kollman, Mindy Spatt, Rob Nolan, Melanie Woodrow, Misty Funk, Lalitha Devi, Margaret Woodside, and Mike Moran—I can't thank you enough for your many hours of work and your thoughtful and invaluable edits. Thank you as well to everyone who allowed me to share your story; your learning will help so many others.

To Kathryn Janus, Hernán Poza, Patricia Simko, Gene Falco, Camilla Brooks, and Michael Keane, thank you for your phenomenal work in teaching and leading Deeper Dating events. Thank you to Ilene Cutler, Silas Cutler-Lockshon, Joe Tripp, Michael Malizia, Mike Moran, Suzanne Gerber, James Young, Hugh Hysell, Beth Greenfield, Lorna Chiu, Milo Shapiro, Tom Tracy, Walker Jones, Sarah-Kay Lacks, Meryl Moss, Sidiki Conde, Deborah Ross, David Schechter, MK Nobilette, Glenn Plaskin, Robyn and Ira Frank, David Singleton, Linda Leonard, Michelle Matlock, Doug Boltson, Don Litwin, Jay Michaelson, Jose Niño, Luis Toca, Nazario Fernández, John Salvato, Perry Brass, Tom Tracy, David Nimmons, Martha Bilski, Lynn Gergen, Dan Diggles, Cathy

Renna, and Gerry Moss, and everyone whose name I somehow didn't mention, for supporting this project, each in your own way. Deep thanks to *Psychology Today*, The Huffington Post, Next Avenue, New York City LGBT Community Center, the Long Island Crisis Center, Easton Mountain, the 92nd Street Y, The JCC in Manhattan, The Garrison Institute, The Rowe Conference Center, The Omega Institute, Nehirim and The Esalen Institute; I am so grateful for your support.

To my mentor, John McNeill, and his husband, Charles Chiarelli—you have shifted the course of our world and have been dear and true friends for many decades; your support means the world to me. Thank you to Conner Middelman-Whitney for your editing insights and for "What is love asking of me?"

Thank you, Jim Sullivan, for being such a fantastic dating coach; Harold Kooden, for your wise help; Shirley Elias, for changing my life. Thank you, Michael Clemente, for creating a home in the world for my soul. To Paramahansa Yogananda, with deepest gratitude.

I feel so lucky to have had the chance to work with Jennifer Urban-Brown, my gracious, patient, and skillful editor at Shambhala. Revision after revision, she remained a wise guide, a compass through challenging terrain and countless sticky choices. To Steven Pomije, Julie Saidenberg, Julia Gaviria, and everyone at Shambhala Publications, I can't believe my amazing good fortune that my book found its home with you. Shambhala's reputation in the field for decency, integrity, and respect for quality writing is more than fully deserved. To my agent, Myrsini Stephanides, thank you so much for believing so fiercely in my work and for being such a committed advocate for it. I'm very grateful. To my clients and workshop participants, thank you for your inspiration. Working with you has been one of the great joys of my life.

Hernán Poza, lifelong true friend, thank you for your rock-solid support throughout this entire Deeper Dating journey, and for the incredible blessing of your friendship. To my parents (who were constantly there for every revision, and whose support and insight made all the difference to me) and to my true friend JoAnne (who also happens to be my loving, generous, and visionary sister!), I simply have no words. How was I lucky enough to end up with three of the most inspiring human beings I know as my family of origin? To Greg, you are living proof of everything I teach and believe in. I love you so much and am so blessed to have found you. Your endless patience, love, and support throughout this entire process meant the world to me. Merrie and Deirdre, you are both such amazing people. David and I and all our family love you and are so fortunate to have you in our lives. David, you are the smile of God to me, and I am forever blessed to be your dad.

Deeper Dating Resources

Thank you so much for your interest in my work. To learn more about my classes, events, workshops, lectures, and webinars, and to find out about Deeper Dating events, please visit my website: www .DeeperDating.com. You will also find a variety of downloads, videos, and other learning materials on this website. I look forward to joining you there!

SAMPLE LETTER TO GIFT CIRCLE HELPERS

Thank you for agreeing to help me in my Gift Circle. I'm asking for your support out of a serious commitment to find healthy intimacy. Please know that I'm only asking my most trusted close friends, family, and supportive professionals to be a part of this process. In telling me the qualities you most value, you will be giving me a tremendous gift. I hope you enjoy doing this, and I hope, too, that you are open to getting the same back. It's not required, but I'd like to give this to you.

The Deeper Dating approach, developed by Ken Page, LCSW, teaches that the wisest path to finding love is by leading with our truest self, the parts of ourselves where we feel the most passion and the most sensitivity. Each of us has points of deepest sensitivity—the places where the roots of our caring go deepest—and they are as unique as our fingerprints. We experience the greatest meaning and the greatest pain in these parts of ourselves, because we feel intuitively that our very identity rests there. Ken Page calls these points Core Gifts because they are like the bone marrow of our psyche, generating not red blood cells but impulses toward intimacy and authentic self-expression.

How do we discover our Core Gifts? According to Page, it's largely through others who see and appreciate them. It has often been stated that we must love ourselves before we can love anyone else, but this is too simplistic: self-love is often learned through being validated precisely in the places where we feel most unsure, most tender.

We all need to be instructed in our deepest gifts.

Most of us do not know enough about what our Core Gifts are and how they affect others. The experience of having these gifts reflected to us can feel like a map emerging from out of the haze, a map of who we are and of the possibilities of who we can become. And when we have a positive sense of who we are, we find the energy to cut through the obstacles, fears, and fogs that separate us from our passion.

Through this process you will be giving this gift to me.

Here's what I am asking you to do by becoming a Gift Circle helper: Think about the qualities that you most love, appreciate, and respect about me. What qualities are unique, what qualities touch and move you the most? Take all the time you need to share them in detail. Be open and take time to search for and find the words and images that really convey these qualities. This process involves only positive feedback. Please do not use this role to criticize or suggest improvements. This Gift Circle is a place for me to learn what you appreciate.

If you are open to it, I'd like to offer the same back to you—your choice. I personally recommend it!

Thanks so much for the gift you are giving me in my journey toward love. I hope it is also a rich experience for you.

Warmly,

MY CORE GIFTS HANDBOOK

This Core Gifts Handbook is a personal user's guide to your own Core Gifts. It will show you how to work with these aspects of your unique "genius" to deepen, speed, and ease your search for love, while enriching your entire life. You can copy this page from here or download it as a PDF from the Deeper Dating website. Enjoy!

1. Describe your Core Gift in one sentence.

2. What image, piece of music or art, or personal memory captures the essence of this gift when it feels most accepted and alive?

3. Name one person in your life who consistently understood, valued, and appreciated this gift. Describe how you feel when your gift is honored in this way.

4. In what type of situations does this gift feel most deprived of oxygen? Describe the pain you feel when this occurs.

5. Describe the ways in which you suppress this gift in your relationships.

6. Describe the way you act out defensively around this gift in your relationships.

7. Describe your deprivational "type": someone who attracts you but can't really honor this particular gift.

8. Describe the kind of person who makes you feel that this gift is valued and appreciated.

9. How would your romantic life change if you shared this gift more fully—with the right people?

10. How might this Core Gift be a pathway into a richer, fuller life for you?

Notes

Introduction

1. Eli Finkel, "The Hack to Save Your Marriage: Eli Finkel at TEDxUChicago," presentation, June 21, 2003, http://tedxtalks.ted.com/video/The-Marriage-Hack-Eli-Finkel-at.

2. DeLois P. Weekes, Sarah H. Kagan, Kelly James, and Naomi Seboni, "The Phenomenon of Hand Holding as a Coping Strategy in Adolescents Experiencing Treatment-Related Pain," *Journal of Pediatric Oncology Nursing* 10, no. 1 (1993): 19–25; doi: 10.1177/104345429301000105; Julianne Holt-Lunstad, Wendy A. Birmingham, and Kathleen C. Light, "Influence of a 'Warm Touch' Support Enhancement Intervention among Married Couples on Ambulatory Blood Pressure, Oxytocin, Alpha Amylase, and Cortisol," *Psychosomatic Medicine* 70, no. 9 (2008): 976–85.

How to Speed Your Path to Love

1. Ashley Montagu, *Touching: The Human Significance of the Skin* (New York: Harper & Row, 1971), 16–42.

2. M. Prince, "Does Active Learning Work? A Review of the Research," *Journal of Engineering Education* 93: 223–31.

STAGE 1
Discover Your Unique Core Gifts

1. David M. Buss, "Human Mate Selection," *American Scientist* 73, no. 1 (January–February 1985): 47–51; www.jstor.org/stable/27853061.

2. Arthur Aron, e-mail message to author, April 7, 2014.

3. Ibid.

1. Your Gift Zone

1. Donald G. Dutton and Arthur P. Aron, "Some Evidence for Heightened Sexual Attraction under Conditions of High Anxiety," *Journal of Personality and Social Psychology* 30, no. 4 (1974): 510–17; doi:10.1037/h0037031.

2. Patricia Simko, e-mail message to author, March 15, 2014.

3. Eugene T. Gendlin, *Focusing* (New York: Bantam Dell, 2007).

2. Your Core Gifts

1. Aubrey L. Gilbert, Terry Regier, Paul Kay, and Richard B. Ivry, "Whorf Hypothesis Is Supported in the Right Visual Field but Not the Left," *Proceedings of the National Academy of Sciences* 103, no. 2 (2006): 489–94; doi:10.1073/pnas.0509868103.

2. Colin Pilkinton-Brodie (writing as Thupten Yarphel), "Universal Altruism: Unbearable Tenderness," *Nectar for the Ear* (blog), January 10, 2012.

3. How to Love Yourself First

1. Edward M. Hallowell, *The Childhood Roots of Adult Happiness: Five Steps to Help Kids Create and Sustain Lifelong Joy* (New York: Ballantine Books, 2002).

2. Jack Kornfield, *A Path with Heart: A Guide through the Perils and Promises of Spiritual Life* (New York: Bantam Books, 1993), 334.

STAGE 2
Recognize Which Attractions Lead to Love and Which Lead to Pain

1. Arthur P. Aron, Edward Melinat, Elaine N. Aron, Robert Darrin Vallone, and Renee J. Bator, "The Experimental Generation of Interpersonal Closeness: A Procedure and Some Preliminary Findings," *Personality and Social Psychology Bulletin* 23, no. 4 (1997): 363–77.

2. Robert Epstein, "How Science Can Help You Fall in Love," *Scientific American Mind* (January–February 2010): 26–33.

4. *Attractions of Inspiration and Attractions of Deprivation*

1. Daniel J. Siegel and Mary Hartzell, *Parenting from the Inside Out: How a Deeper Self-Understanding Can Help You Raise Children Who Thrive* (New York: Penguin Press, 2004), 185–94.
2. Kathryn Janus, e-mail message to author, September 23, 2013.
3. Arthur Aron, "Why Do We Fall in Love?" *How Stuff Works* (website), May 10, 2005.
4. Eli J. Finkel and P. E. Eastwick, "Interpersonal Attraction: In Search of a Theoretical Rosetta Stone," in *Handbook of Personality and Social Psychology: Interpersonal Relations and Group Processes*, edited by J. A. Simpson and J. F. Dovidio, 393–420 (Washington, D.C.: American Psychological Association, in press).

6. *Tapping Your Deepest Roots*

1. David E. Greenan, e-mail message to author, May 5, 2013.
2. Arielle Ford, *The Soulmate Secret* (New York: HarperCollins, 2008; Kindle Edition), 9.

STAGE 3
Learn the Skills of Deeper Dating

1. Eli J. Finkel and Paul Eastwick, "Should You Play Hard to Get?" *The Attractionologists* (blog), July 5, 2008; e-mail message to author, April 29, 2014.

7. *The Seven Skills of Deeper Dating*

1. Wendy Widom (president of the website *Families in the Loop*), e-mail message to author, March 23, 2014.
2. Eli J. Finkel and Paul Eastwick, "Should You Play Hard to Get?" *The Attractionologists* (blog), July 5, 2008.
3. Daniel Goleman, *Social Intelligence: The New Science of Human Relationships* (New York: Bantam Dell, 2006), 4–5.

4. Keith Ferrazzi, *Never Eat Alone: And Other Secrets to Success, One Relationship at a Time* (New York: Bantam Doubleday Dell, 2005).

8. A *Deeper Dating Guide to Finding Love*

1. Jamie Cat Callan, e-mail message to author, July 22, 2013; *French Women Don't Sleep Alone: Pleasurable Secrets to Finding Love* (New York: Kensington Publishing, 2009).
2. Sarah Bridge, "Do Singles Events Make You Feel More Single?" *HuffPost Lifestyle, United Kingdom* (blog), August 28, 2012.

STAGE 4
Cultivate Lasting Love

1. Dan Schawbel, "Brené Brown: How Vulnerability Can Make Our Lives Better," *Forbes*, April 21, 2013, www.forbes.com/sites/danschawbel/2013/04/21/brene-brown-how-vulnerability-can-make-our-lives-better.
2. Brené Brown, *Daring Greatly: How the Courage to Be Vulnerable Transforms the Way We Live, Love, Parent, and Lead* (New York: Gotham Books, 2012).

11. *Cultivating Sexual and Romantic Attraction to People Who are Good for You*

1. "Moth," *Neuroscience for Kids* (website), University of Washington, http://faculty.washington.edu/chudler/amaze.html.
2. Harville Hendrix, *Getting the Love You Want: A Guide for Couples, 20th Anniversary Edition* (New York: Henry Holt, 2007).
3. Ibid.
4. Robert Epstein, "How Science Can Help You Fall in Love," *Scientific American Mind* (January–February 2010): 26–33.
5. Elaine Aron, *The Highly Sensitive Person in Love: Understanding and Managing Relationships When the World Overwhelms You* (New York: Crown Publishing Group, 2009; Kindle Edition), 110.
6. Irene Tsapelas, Arthur Aron, and Terri Orbuch, "Marital Boredom Now Predicts Less Satisfaction Nine Years Later," *Psychological Science* 20, no. 5 (2009): 543–45.

7. Craig Malkin, "Five Proven Ways to Revive Romance on Valentine's Day," *Psychology Today* (February 12, 2011).

8. Uwe Hartmann, "Sigmund Freud and His Impact on Our Understanding of Male Sexual Dysfunction," *Journal of Sexual Medicine* 6, no. 8 (2009): 2332–39.

12. *Being Loved into Fullness*

1. George E. Vaillant, *Triumphs of Experience: The Men of the Harvard Grant Study* (Cambridge, Mass.: The Belknap Press of Harvard University Press, 2012, Kindle Edition).

Index

About the Author

Ken Page, LCSW, is a psychotherapist, lec-
turer, and recognized expert on the search
for intimacy. He is the author of the popular *Psychology Today* blog *Finding Love*.
His insights on dating and the deeper skills
of intimacy have touched hundreds of
thousands of readers. He has been featured
in *O, The Oprah Magazine*; the *New York
Times*; WPIX-TV; and *Cosmopolitan*.

©Mark Milch

Ken is the founder of Deeper Dating, an event in which single
people meet in an environment that encourages self-discovery and
positive interaction. A dynamic speaker, he also lectures and leads
workshops and online classes on intimacy, self-acceptance, and the
search for love. Ken and his family live on Long Island, New York.
For more information on his classes and events or to inquire about
speaking engagements, please visit DeeperDating.com.